The Making and Remaking
of the Good Friday Agreement

THE MAKING AND REMAKING OF THE GOOD FRIDAY AGREEMENT

Paul Bew

The Liffey Press

Published by
The Liffey Press
Ashbrook House 10 Main Street
Raheny, Dublin 5, Ireland
www.theliffeypress.com

© 2007 Paul Bew

A catalogue record of this book is
available from the British Library.

ISBN 978-1-905785-17-9

Printed in the Republic of Ireland by Colour Books

ABOUT THE AUTHOR

Paul Bew is Professor of Irish Politics at Queens University Belfast. He is a member of the Royal Irish Academy and the author of *Ireland: The Politics of Enmity, 1790-2007* in the Oxford History of Modern Europe series. In February 2007 he was appointed a cross-bench peer to the House of Lords.

Acknowledgements
The author would like to thank the many editors and newspapers involved in the commissioning of these pieces for their permission to re-publish.

CONTENTS

Contents

Contents

Contents

To the memory of Arthur Green

TIMELINE

31 August 1994 – IRA ceasefire is announced: "Recognising the potential of the current situation and in order to enhance the democratic peace process and underline our definitive commitment to its success, the leadership of Oglaigh na h'Eireann have decided that as of midnight, Wednesday 31 August, there will be a complete cessation of military operations. All our units have been instructed accordingly ..."

22 February 1995 – British and Irish governments publish the documents "Frameworks for the Future"; designed to ensure the continuation of the IRA ceasefire, the document has a green tone unacceptable to unionists.

9 February 1996 – IRA ends its ceasefire. A bomb at Canary Wharf Tower in London kills two men and injures more than 100 others.

1 May 1997 – A landslide New Labour victory in the British general election.

19 July 1997 – The IRA announces restoration of its 1994 ceasefire.

17 September 1997 – Ulster Unionist party enters multi-party negotiations including Sinn Féin.

10 April 1998 – The Belfast Agreement or Good Friday Agreement is achieved based on the support of the Ulster Unionist party and its allies delivering a majority of the Ulster electorate and the SDLP delivering a majority of the nationalist electorate.

2 December 1999 – The actual establishment of power-sharing institutions including Sinn Féin.

11 February 2000 – The British government suspends power-sharing executive because of IRA failure to move on arms issues.

5 May 2000 – IRA promises to put its arms "completely and verifiably beyond use".

27 May 2000 – Power-sharing institutions return.

23 May 2001 – Trimble lodges a letter with the Speaker of the Northern Irish Assembly, resigning as First Minister from 1 July 2001, if by then – on the other side of a general election – the IRA had not begun to decommission. In the June general election, the SDLP was eclipsed by Sinn Féin.

July 2001 – Weston Park negotiations: on 19 July, the British and Irish governments publish their joint communiqué, in which arms was only one aspect of the negotiation and the last mentioned item. Public perception was that Sinn Féin rather than the Ulster Unionists emerged the stronger from the negotiations, which also gave a strong boost to the enquiry cultures.

11 September 2001 – Terrorist attacks on World Trade Centre in New York and Pentagon in Washington.

26 October 2001 – The IRA announces that it had begun the process of decommissioning. Trimble responds by return to governing with Sinn Féin.

4 October 2002 – "Stormontgate" crisis. Power-sharing institutions collapse amidst claims of a republican spy ring at the heart of government.

17 October 2002 – Blair speech, Harbour Commissioners, Belfast. Blair argued that the IRA's latent threat of violence had become counter-productive. It was time for "acts of completion", time for the IRA to make the break from its violent past. "The crunch is the crunch. There is no parallel track left. The fork on the road has come." There were to be no more grinding "inch by inch" negotiations. Blair dismissed those on the unionist side who perpetually trashed the agreement as "malign whisperers". Remarkably, in his definition of the "new future" enjoyed by Northern Ireland since 1998, Blair noted that "People who used to advocate the murder of British ministers and security forces would be working with them". Blair called for an end to all paramilitary activity.

1 May 2003 – The Joint Declaration. The two governments publish a joint declaration setting out the steps to be taken by them in anticipation of an acceptable IRA statement: "We need to see an immediate, full and permanent cessation of all paramilitary activity, including military attacks, training, intelligence gathering, acquisition of arms, punishment beatings and attacks and involvement in riots" (para 13).

September 2003 – Private handshake between Gerry Adams and David Trimble: negotiations designed to re-start the executive intensify.

21 October 2003 – The Hillsborough Fiasco. The government announces assembly elections in November. Gerry Adams issues a statement avoiding any reference to the ending of paramilitary activities of targeting, training and punishment beatings that had been mentioned in the joint declaration. General de Chastelain announces that there has been further IRA decommissioning, but he offers no inventory of the arms which had been destroyed. David Trimble calls off the deal he has been negotiating, which had attempted to restore the power-sharing executive. The DUP emerge as the strongest unionist party in the November election.

8 December 2004 – Collapse of "Comprehensive Agreement" – the text negotiated by Sinn Féin and the DUP for a return to government.

20 December 2004 – Northern Bank robbery: armed men steal £26 million. In January the Chief Constable of the PSNI declares that the IRA was responsible.

28 July 2005 – IRA formally declares its campaign over.

26 September 2005 – General de Chastelain announces that the IRA has decommissioned the great bulk of its remaining weaponry.

6 April 2006 – In his Armagh speech, Tony Blair sets absolute deadline for the achievement of devolution, 24 November 2006

11-13 October 2006 – St Andrews Agreement: an agreement between the British and Irish governments, but Dr Paisley signals crucial willingness to share power with Sinn Féin if they accept policing. A new assembly election is announced for early March 2007.

7 March 2007 – DUP and Sinn Féin emerge as victors in assembly election; anti-agreement campaigners fare poorly.

8 May 2007 – DUP and Sinn Féin agree to form new power-sharing government of Northern Ireland on this date.

INTRODUCTION

THE ARTICLES PRESENTED HERE CONSTITUTE an argumentative survey of the Northern Irish peace process, from the IRA ceasefire of 1994 to the agreement to form the DUP–Sinn Féin government of Northern Ireland in May 2007. The key theme of British and Irish government policy since the early 1990s was the inclusion of the so-called "extremes". This marked a shift from the policy of the Anglo-Irish Agreement of 1985, which was aimed, above all, at boosting constitutional nationalism. The governments plotted a torturous, controversial course, which at many times looked as if it was doomed to failure; nonetheless, in the end – at a high local political price – the basic objectives of London and Dublin were achieved.

What is the point of reprinting essays, several of them containing judgements which are either flawed or became redundant, as circumstances changed or political personalities reinvented themselves – essays which after all certainly reflect the passions of the time? Yet there is a point. Today the Good Friday Agreement of 1998 appears to be secure. The legislation announcing its return has passed the Westminster parliament. Not one of the 108 members of the Stormont Assembly elected in March 2007 has a fundamental objection to the Good Friday Agreement template – only slightly revised by the St Andrews negotiations of October 2006. But the essays presented here are permeated by a sense of the precariousness of the whole venture. From the moment of the IRA ceasefire in 1994, the author is clearly committed to this project but many of the articles feel as if they are written against the tide. This book therefore constitutes a particular angle of vision – but without the opportunity for mature reflection or, to put it another way, the distortions of hindsight.

The essays are haunted by a question: were the British and Irish governments right to prioritise the Adams leadership and its capacity to control the republican movement over the democratic nationalists of the SDLP or the moderate unionists of the Ulster Unionist Party? Was it really possible, as John Hume has pointed out, for the IRA to return to war after the all-Ireland referendum underpinning the Agreement in 1998? Was it possible after the Omagh bomb outrage of 1998? Was it remotely conceivable after the terrorist attacks in New York and Washington on September 11, 2001? After all, despite the best efforts of the British, Irish and American governments in, for example, calling an election in highly unpropitious circumstances in 2003, the republican movement was denied participation in a Northern Ireland executive from 2002 to 2007 but did not return to war. In the end, also, it delivered both decommissioning and acceptance of policing without enduring a serious split.

It may be appropriate to add one further comment. In September 2001 David Trimble came close to a decisive victory, when IRA decommissioning was announced. I have been told by a member of the DUP's Assembly Party that this development provoked a serious debate within the DUP, with modernisers urging a reduction in hostility to the institutions of the Good Friday Agreement, while traditionalists, who won the argument, insisted that the full hostility be maintained. In the course of 2002, Trimble's position steadily weakened. In the spring of that year, the US State Department held a seminar in Washington devoted to the topic of how best to help moderate unionism; it ended, significantly, on a note of speculation about a DUP–Sinn Féin deal ("Anger over Secret North Conference", *Irish Voice*, 17 April 2002). By the late summer of 2002, it became commonplace to meet officials

2

of the British, Irish and US governments who had begun to believe that the future lay with a Sinn Féin–DUP deal.

In the end, such a deal took five years. Mr Blair, in the end, did manage to bring it about on his watch with only days to spare; many of the officials involved in the process (including British) assumed it would have to await a new prime minister. The old questions of 1993-2007 are now resolved. Will the IRA declare its war over and start an evolution towards being an old boys club? Will unionists accept a power-sharing plus an Irish dimension settlement? We now know – apparently at least – the answers to these questions.

We are now facing a distinctive new set of questions. What are the implications for the long-term development of unionist politics of Dr Paisley's belated conversion to power-sharing and compromise? Will the new executive be stable and/or reconciling? Nor will all the old questions go away entirely. The ancient problem of Northern Irish governance still remains. It is never quite the end of history, "Irish style". The Irish government has a formal voice on behalf of the Catholic and nationalist minority, while the British government believes itself to have an equal responsibility to both communities. The potential imbalance here may yet have unpredictable consequences. But the fact remains that we are on new terrain, and a particular type of break (ambiguous as it always is) has been made with the historic pattern.

The new questions will focus on new issues. Given the complete identity of policy, why two unionist parties? Will the more parochial form of unionism represented by the DUP lead to a diminution of the resonance of unionism's case within the rest of a United Kingdom, much influenced by a new surge of Scottish nationalism? Will Sinn Féin's attempt to establish an interactive north-south political strategy, in which success in one part of the island reinforces it in another, actually work? Does it have the capacity to speed up Irish unity? It will, in later generations, be for others, no doubt more objective and detached, to reach a judgement on the meaning of these events. What is presented here is a "first draft of history", the effort to catch – in a moment which is always unrepeatable – the political meaning of events as they unfold in front of the observers' eyes.

The end of this distinct phase of Irish history coincides with the end of the Blair era: the second British prime minister (after Bonar Law) to be of Ulster Protestant parentage and, like John Major, to be technically eligible for the Irish football team. We have already reached the point where novels evoking the Blair era are coming thick and fast. But so far, no novelist has been brave enough to imagine a sunny Sunday morning in Islington in the early summer of 1997, in which Tony Blair contemplates that his last effective alliance will be with Dr Ian Paisley. But so it has been, and it poses profound questions about Tony Blair's role in Ireland.

There are basically three interpretations in print. One, associated with Michael Portillo, sees this essentially as Paisley's victory over a vacillating Blair. Paisley stood firm on decommissioning and, above all, on the need for public republican acceptance of policing, whilst Blair was ambiguous on these issues until very late in the day. In this analysis, Paisley is the last man standing, about to enter the pomp of office and power just as Tony Blair leaves it, having outlasted Harold Wilson, Edward Heath, Jim Callaghan, Margaret Thatcher and John Major as well. There is another view, associated with some in the now marginalised centre parties of Northern Ireland, who originally gave Mr Blair his Good Friday arrangement in 1998. Seamus Mallon, the former SDLP Deputy First Minister of Northern Ireland, has been particularly sharp in his criticisms. In this version, the collapse of the centre parties becomes almost a function of a deliberate Downing Street strategy of fostering the extremes. The argument here is that Northern Ireland has achieved not so much power-sharing as power-splitting and internal balkanisation in 2007. The changes to the Belfast Agreement achieved at St Andrews – small though they are – symbolically remove the cross-community element in the election of the first minister, whilst other changes, designed to reduce controversial ministerial autonomy, may lead to gridlock.

Finally, there is the view of Downing Street itself and of some supporters in the media. In this view, everything is for the best in the best of all possible worlds. A dramatic and unexpected reconciliation has been achieved, and it is even whispered that the new politicians of the DUP and Sinn Féin who will dominate the governance of Northern Ireland are more workman-like and pragmatic than their cranky predecessors in the SDLP and the UUP. This last interpretation might be called the triumphant Blairite teleology of the peace process.

In fact, there are problems with all three interpretations. While it is only fair to say that Dr Paisley was not apparently cowed by threats of Plan B (increased British-Irish co-operation) and made his decision for essentially positive reasons,[1] it remains the case that he is now, in fact, on the verge of becoming co-equal premier of Northern Ireland with Martin McGuinness. The deputy first minister of Northern Ireland is not a John Prescott-like figure, stepping in when the prime minister is on holiday etc, but half of the collective political first citizen of Northern Ireland. In this, as in so many other respects, Dr Paisley has accepted the political structures of the Good Friday Agreement, structures which he and his party condemned for years as being incompatible with the safety of the union. Today, Dr Paisley is about to enter office, asserting as strongly as David Trimble did that this deal embodies the end of traditional Irish republicanism. In that sense, this is a posthumous political triumph for Lord Trimble, but it is not the triumph over Mr Blair imagined by some commentators.

---

[1] This apparently goes against the theme of Dr Paisley's recent BBC interview: "The British government threatened me. I was frightened. I was frightened for my country" (*Irish Times*, 6 April 2007). In this interview, Dr Paisley is concerned to meet the challenge that he gratuitously betrayed fundamental principles of his career: as Jim Allister pointed out, "Plan B" was never seriously discussed by DUP party officers. Senior officials are more inclined to believe that Dr Paisley was driven by a desire to bring about a positive outcome to the talks.

What are we to make of the angst of the SDLP and Ulster Unionists, who did so much for Mr Blair between 1998 and 2001? The first point to be acknowledged is that the long-term social and demographic indicators were against both parties, regardless of any decision taken by the prime minister. Furthermore, once the sectarian dynamic was unleashed by Sinn Féin's electoral victory in 2001, it was always likely that the Protestant community would reply by voting DUP in 2003. Nonetheless, a problem remains about Mr Blair's management of the process. As late as early 2005, the IRA still felt it worth its while to threaten the British government with a return to war. The implication is clear. Despite Mr Blair telling Frank Millar in the *Irish Times* on 8 November 2002 that the "world had changed" since 9/11 and that terrorism was no longer an option for the IRA, that movement perceived a continuing weakness and fear in the British state. It allowed it to monopolise the negotiating position – as Peter Mandelson has recently confirmed in the *Guardian* of 13 March 2007 – at the expense of the moderate parties, who thus lost face and support in front of their own electorates. How much was the government influenced by its own fear, not of a sustained IRA return to violence, but of events such as Canary Wharf, which would have been massively embarrassing to the government itself?

Finally, there is the more upbeat view that everything has worked out for the best. There can be no question that Mr Blair devoted an enormous amount of time for Northern Ireland, and the fact that it is a better place today than it was in 1997 must, in part, be due to his labours. He has persisted where others would have flagged. His very lack of interest in long-term constitutional options and processes – which some say has been harmful in a wider British context – has worked to his advantage in Northern Ireland. He has been concerned simply to work within the parameters of the Good Friday Agreement and to bring about its implementation in full. This, in effect, he has now done, and it is an achievement to be respected: it is also, intriguingly, a less anti-unionist outcome than many expected when the scale of the Labour landslide became clear in 1997.

The political future of Northern Ireland remains, however, an open one. It will inevitably be touted as a model for peacemakers worldwide. It is, in fact, a unique and specific story – the story of the difficulties faced by a liberal democratic state, weakened by historic guilt about its record in Ireland, dealing with terrorism within its own borders.

ᬓ ᬓ ᬓ

MOLYNEAUX MUST SHOW
IMAGINATIVE GENEROSITY
The Times, 1 September 1994

The big political and economic facts of life favour the Ulster Unionists. Albert Reynolds openly admitted during his St Patrick's Day trip to the United States, for example, that Northern Ireland required the British subvention at the current level for many years to come. Presumably it is partly in consequence of this insight that the Irish prime minister also observed that he did not expect to see a united Ireland in his lifetime.

Yet, why is it that when the Ulster Unionists announce, as they did at their recent conference, that they are attempting a mission to outline the unionist case before the world, that the heart sinks and the mind knows that the mission is unlikely to succeed?

In Harold McCusker's phrase after the signing of the Anglo-Irish Agreement, Irish unionism has been reduced to the status of an activity which can go on in private between two consenting adults. Tom King, the former Northern Ireland Secretary, averred that he was a unionist; Sir Patrick Mayhew feels it safer to be a "Northern Irelandist".

How has it happened that Irish unionism has come to be stripped of so many elements of its public respectability and

credibility? At first sight, it is surprising. In many important respects, the union has been – especially in economic and social
terms – a success for the Irish people who have lived under it
since the 1850s. Why then do those who defend the union feel,
quite rightly, that they are on the defensive?

The problem begins with Gladstone's peremptory and ill-fated
conversion to home rule in 1886. Even though Gladstone is later
prepared to consider exclusion for the north east, the prospect
opens up for Irish nationalism that a British prime minister might
place all of Ireland under a home rule parliament.

In reaction, something starts to happen to the argument for the
union: it ceases to be a thesis (on the face of it a perfectly respectable one) that the future of Ireland as a whole would be a brighter
one within the union. It becomes, understandably, as that lucid
organ of high unionism, the *Quarterly Review*, pointed out, a more
limited case for Ulster unionist self-determination.

It is remarkable how little Sir Edward Carson says about the
general case – which he profoundly believed in – during the third
home rule crisis of 1912-14. It is remarkable how often he says instead that every argument which points towards special treatment
for Irish nationalists is also an argument for special treatment for
Ulster unionists.

As the liberal unionist *Ballymoney Free Press* dolefully expressed it: "The statement of unionist Ulster is that it merely
wants to be let alone ... unfortunately, since Satan entered the
Garden of Eden, good people will not be let alone".

It was hardly an inspiring clarion call to outsiders. Yet, even at
this level, the argument had its merits and achieved cogent expression in the speeches of Bonar Law, Balfour and Chamberlain
or the writing of Dicey. The sheer intellectual lustre of the unionist case is worth recalling: Cambridge University, for example,
returned successively as MPs two great Irish scientists, Sir Robert
Ball and Sir Joseph Larmor, to articulate the scientific community's opposition to home rule.

But by 1914 religion on "the mainland" was essentially a private matter. In Ireland, on the other hand, it became linked ever more intensely with political allegiance.

As political Protestantism, a phenomenon embracing both nineteenth-century English parties, declined in the rest of the UK, Ulster Protestants appeared as an increasingly "uncool", vulgar parody of Britishness. Matters were made worse by the region's relative economic decline and growing dependence on the centre after 1920. Only Irish neutrality in the second world war allowed a brief unionist return to popularity in London.

James Molyneaux therefore has never had the option of playing the "heroic" Carson role. At times in the mid-1980s he seemed content merely to manage decline, though it is fair to say that in more recent years he has harvested small but significant gains (a Northern Ireland Select Committee for example) at every turn. He has held, however, the ground which mattered and protected the British citizenship of his supporters.

If peace has really come, it will be open to him to show unusual imagination and generosity. He should not forget that in February 1926 even Sir James Craig, a tough unionist prime minister, felt able to offer broad north-south co-operation in the name of a common Irish patriotism.

ೞ ೞ ೞ

ULSTER: WHO WILL GIVE GROUND?
The Times, 2 September 1994

It requires a definite leap of the imagination – a constitutional conference on the future of Northern Ireland, involving Ian Paisley, Gerry Adams, John Hume, and Jim Molyneaux. Frankly, even after the IRA's dramatic declaration of a "complete cessation" of violence, the odds are still against this configuration. Doubts about the "permanent" cessation of IRA violence will have been increased by Mitchell McLaughlin's statement yesterday that the IRA ceasefire was "doomed" if the British government reacted in a negative manner. Mr McLaughlin, after all, is usually seen as one of the Sinn Féin doves.

Even if the peace holds, Ian Paisley will in all probability never want to sit down with Gerry Adams. Nevertheless, we have in the last two days moved appreciably closer to the prospect of a rather overcrowded and ill-tempered conference.

So what is the possibility of a political settlement based on such a dialogue? At this point it may be worth looking at the Mayhew talks process of 1992 – often wrongly dismissed as a predictably futile failure. As these talks came to an end on 9 November 1992, the Ulster unionists – all too belatedly – tabled a series of proposals. These include a Bill of Rights for Northern Ireland to protect minorities; nationalists would have a "meaningful role" in the administration of Northern Ireland; and given "the reality that a significant proportion of the Roman Catholic community in Northern Ireland may aspire to a united Ireland", there should be an "Inter-Irish Relations Committee" formally linking members of the Ulster Assembly and the Irish parliament.

In return, the Ulster Unionists asked Dublin "to define a means whereby the aggressive and irredentist articles 2 and 3 in the Irish constitution would be removed". From the SDLP they asked "a de facto commitment to a Northern Ireland where all constitutional parties would be able to play a meaningful role". Nonetheless, this dramatic move did not stop the failure of the negotiations, much to the disappointment of the British government. Ironically, British pressure on unionism since the Anglo-Irish Agreement appeared to have worked: at the price of considerable local destabilisation. During the talks Ulster Unionists had made the symbolic trip to Dublin at which the Paisleyite Democratic Unionists had balked. They had also moved significantly inside the talks process itself, in effect conceding in principle both power-sharing and an Irish dimension – but this movement by the unionists did not lead to a deal with the SDLP.

The SDLP remained wedded throughout the process to its original "European model" proposal, which suggested one European Community, one Dublin and one London nominee on a six-man Northern Ireland executive commission. Moreover, the proposed parliamentary assembly was to be modelled on the European parliament; that is to say, it was to be a largely advisory body, without a legislative role and with no effective control over the executive. These proposals predictably found no favour with the Ulster Unionists and Democratic Unionists; less predictably, they found no favour with the non-sectarian moderate Alliance party or the British government. Few observers in Brussels believed that the European Community was anxious for such a role. The talks were also deadlocked on the issue of articles 2 and 3 of the Irish constitution.

As the talks collapsed, press briefings by the Northern Ireland Office referred to the possibility of a change in SDLP attitudes when the ordinary membership realised how much was on offer. Such a development was, however, rather unlikely.

The Anglo-Irish Agreement has created a context in which it has become logical – almost compellingly so – for constitutional nationalists (and the British Labour party) to argue for a form of joint authority, perhaps with a European dimension. It has to be understood, too, that the collapse of the 1974 power-sharing experiment makes it very difficult for the SDLP to trust unionists.

There is perhaps a new subtlety in political discourse. Mainstream unionists now concede ground on power-sharing and the Irish dimension, while constitutional nationalists aim for joint authority rather than a united Ireland. The Alliance party even praised the DUP for supporting a system which could evolve into power-sharing – while the SDLP repeatedly insisted that "equality of esteem" meant an executive role for the Irish government in the north.

There is currently much speculation about a possible constitutional traditional "trade-off" between articles 2 and 3 of the Irish constitution, which express a claim over Northern Ireland, and section 75 of the Government of Ireland Act of 1920, which expresses the UK parliament's sovereignty over Northern Ireland. Some unnecessarily exotic formulations have been proposed in this context – but, in substance, this proposal is not without merit. The sharpest legal mind in the Ulster Unionist parliamentary party, David Trimble, has pointed out in the latest *Parliamentary Brief* that the legislation governing Northern Ireland's place within the UK is the Act of Union of 1800 and the 1973 Constitutional Act.

A NIO statement of last Saturday seemed to echo this in a rather uncanny way. Many moderate unionists are understandably upset by the notion of any tinkering with the 1920 Act, but there is, perhaps, a greater good at stake which permits a constitutional restructuring based on the concept of consent.

There is a sense (but only at present a superficial one) in which the outline of a settlement is already in place. Responsibility-sharing in the north combined with north-south institutions precisely calibrated so that they may be seen to be based on the principle of mutual co-operation. For Irish nationalists this offers the possibility of a level playing field on which they – as opposed to the London government, as in Sinn Féin's rather peculiar demand – might attempt to persuade unionists of the benefits of Irish unity. For unionists it offers the possibility, at least, of stability in the province.

In many ways it is an imperfect arrangement, but it now appears to be the only possible benign outcome: despite the greater theoretical value of other proposals, it may well be that there is not enough purely Irish good will – either nationalist or unionist – to achieve such a settlement. This does not mean, however, that the status quo becomes in some sense "intolerable": there is little likelihood of any crisis of direct rule, unless provoked by London.

If there is to be a new talks process, it is perhaps worth making some pointers about structure. There were far too many delegates present the last time. The result was often messy and rhetorical. Mr Molyneaux's taste for "high wire acts" was understandably rather discouraged. It should not be assumed, however, that moderate unionists (in a context of peace) will not be able to talk to Sinn Féin people; they already have to do it in Northern Ireland's councils. It is British government ministers who refuse to speak to the republicans.

Most important of all is the approval of the political leaders. If the peace holds, John Hume will achieve a genuinely Parnellian stature in Irish history – his achievement would perhaps be even greater. But he has not only to quote Parnell's Belfast May 1891 speech on the need to conciliate Irish unionists but also to act on its spirit: so far, he has not found it easy to do that.

For the record, Parnell said: "I have to say this, that it is the duty of the nationalist majority to leave no stone unturned, no means unused, to conciliate the reasonable or unreasonable prejudices of the unionist minority ... every Irish patriot has always recognised ... that until the religious prejudices of the minority, whether reasonable or unreasonable, are conciliated ... Ireland can never enjoy perfect freedom, Ireland can never be united; so long ... as there is this important minority who consider, rightly or wrongly – I believe and feel sure wrongly – that the concession of legitimate freedom to Ireland means harm and damage to them, either to their spiritual or their temporal interests, the work of building up an independent Ireland will have upon it a fatal clog and a fatal drag".

In recent weeks it has been up to other members of his parliamentary party to defend the honour of constitutional nationalism; even yesterday Mr Hume roundly insisted that unionists could not trust the British government – even though Mr Molyneaux's decision to trust Mr Major was painfully evident. It requires also the unionists to build substantially on the greater flexibility displayed in the 1992 talks. The prize is great. Northern Ireland regularly obtains the best A-level results in the UK, but these people are so often lost in the "brain drain". Given a decent settlement, it might just be possible to halt the regional decline.

CB CB CB

MODEST REALITIES LURK BEHIND ALL-EMBRACING RHETORIC OF DOCUMENT
The Times, 23 February 1995

Has the government got it right with its new Northern Ireland initiative? Clearly, yesterday's proposals were not in support of a classic joint authority, though the Anglo-Irish Agreement's inter-governmental conference remains a key part of the scene. Clearly, too, the government is seeking the definitive end of the Irish territorial claim to the north – though significantly no definite wording appears to have been agreed.

The Framework Document meets none of Sinn Féin's demands for a timetable for withdrawal. Yet, most unionists were angry yesterday, and the impression persists that the government may have miscalculated. How has this happened? The core belief of Ulster unionism is clear: "It is better to be separated from the rest of Ireland than from Great Britain". There is a definite implication: unionist politicians are unlikely to make major sacrifices to bring about a local assembly if the price is to give Dublin an unacceptably large role in the north. Hence yesterday's proposal for a northern assembly will not, in itself, calm unionist fears about the content of the document.

Furthermore, there is as yet no hard evidence that unionist politicians are out of touch with their community. Most unionists give power-sharing as a preferred option, but only 12 per cent opt for power-sharing plus an Irish dimension. Both governments will hope for a shift.

The key problem is the nature of the proposed Irish dimension. The Framework Document proposes a new north-south body that would have executive functions at the outset in, for example, the areas of EC programmes and initiatives, marketing and promotion abroad and culture and heritage. The appearance of the last item indicates the depth of change since the Sunningdale experiment in 1974. Then – as the documentation shows – a senior UK official insisted privately: "For a government to hand over its functions in respect of … culture to some international authority would be to abdicate its basic responsibility".

But behind these executive functions are a range of functions subject to harmonisation, defined as "both sides using their best endeavours to reach agreement on a common policy". These include aspects of agriculture and fisheries, industrial development, consumer affairs, transport, energy, trade, health, social welfare, education and economic policy – sensitive matters for middle-class and working-class unionist opinion. In addition, further functions are subject to consultation.

This looks like a bureaucratic fantasia designed to appeal to the Sinn Féin leadership anxious to begin a long march through the institutions towards the united Ireland. Yet, it may well be that some very modest realities lurk behind the apparently all-embracing scenario outlined in the text.

The last time harmonisation of social welfare was seriously suggested was in 1984, when Clive Soley MP, then a Labour party spokesman on Ulster, called for pensions and other social welfare entitlements for Northern Ireland citizens to be mailed from Dublin, but paid for by the British Exchequer. The Dublin postmark was seen as a means to break down unionist working-class prejudice against the southern neighbour.

Are we entitled to believe that anything like this is intended this time? Certainly not. After the leak to *The Times*, it became clear that abstract concepts like "harmonisation" needed to be clarified. In a very significant late presentational change, paragraph 33 offers a vitally important translation of that frightening term. Harmonisation in education, for example, reduces to "mutual recognition of teacher qualifications, co-operative venture in higher education, in teacher training, in education for mutual understanding and in education for specialised needs". That is all perfectly sensible but hardly very exciting.

There is less to some of this framework rhetoric than meets the eye. The Prime Minister explained this well at his press conference, and the Northern Ireland educational world relaxed. Why has he not done a similar job in private with James Molyneaux?

The unionists need to be convinced the north-south body will develop only with their agreement. There is no point in a hectoring approach. The people of Northern Ireland need time and space to consider these documents objectively.

 appears: CЗ CЗ CЗ

GIVING WAY TO THE IRA OVER ARMS
The Times, 24 May 1995

For all the inevitable air of pantomime, Sir Patrick Mayhew's Washington meeting with Gerry Adams is probably the only way to prevent a public relations disaster. It may very well be that the idea of sending the Secretary of State at all is based on an overestimation of the purely economic value of this conference on investment, but once the decision to send Sir Patrick was taken, the meeting with the Sinn Féin president was inevitable.

So far, American economic commitment to Northern Ireland has been disappointing in real terms; analogies with the Marshall aid package are ridiculous. The current level of American aid to Northern Ireland annually barely outstrips the gifts of rich individuals to universities in the Irish Republic. If there is a dividend, it is more likely to be political: the British government will hope, against hope, that the Adams-Mayhew meeting will help to initiate meaningful discussions about arms between Michael Ancram and Martin McGuinness.

More worryingly, the Washington conference may be used as a platform for Dublin's strident policy of economic "harmonisation". Ron Brown, the troubled American Commerce Secretary, has apparently supported the idea of harmonising corporation tax north and south at the much lower level that currently prevails in the Republic. This is a characteristic Dublin theme, but it ignores the crucial importance of a uniform tax rate within the United Kingdom. In this respect, the Framework Document did not visibly concede any ground, for the uniform rate is essential to the status of the province as an integral part of the United Kingdom.

Once again, a unionist leader, friendly to the British government, has been badly used. James Molyneaux has devoted much effort recently to trying to build around Sir Patrick a *cordon sanitaire* – but this has now been decisively breached. The visible snubbing of the unionist leader can only increase the chances of Robert McCartney QC – an arch-critic of Mr Molyneaux's style – in the forthcoming North Down by-election.

On arms, there is no doubt that the two governments have now gone back on their words. On the day of the Downing Street Declaration in December 1993, Dick Spring, the Irish Foreign Minister, told the Dáil: "We are talking about a permanent cessation of violence, and we are talking about a handing up of arms, with the insistence that it would not be a case of 'we are on a temporary cessation of violence to see what the political process offers'." The two governments agreed that there could be no room for equivocation. This message was strongly supported by John Bruton, then the leader of the opposition.

On 1 June 1994, lest anyone had forgotten, Mr Spring used precisely the same language: "There will have to be a verification of the handing over of arms. As I have said publicly, there is little point in attempting to bring people into political dialogue on the basis of giving it a try, and if it does not work returning to the bomb and the bullet ... it has to be permanent, and there must be evidence of it. There will obviously have to be a precise means of establishing the commitment to use exclusively peaceful methods, and that obviously has to be decided and agreed by both governments. There can be no participation by Sinn Féin-IRA in political discussions with either government until they have made a firm commitment that violence has ended".

These speeches clearly demonstrate the falsity of the claim made by republicans – and some fellow travellers in Fianna Fáil – that the handing over of arms was not raised before the ceasefire. But they also show slippage by both governments in two areas: ministers, including Sir Patrick Mayhew, have met Sinn Féin before decommissioning, and many observers believe that a symbolic surrender of some arms will satisfy both governments.

It is only fair to add that the other side has changed its tune too. There is some evidence of a melting of hard-core intransigent republican ideology in Northern Ireland. When Jim Gibney, a senior republican, talks of coming to terms with the "positive aspects" of the Britishness of the unionists, we are entering new territory. At the weekend, Mr Gibney talked of a need for a new language of compromise: a united Ireland remained his "preferred option", but, he added, "there are other options. We will examine them carefully ... We will consider any political model designed to accommodate the special characteristics of the Irish people which history has handed down to us".

This is very encouraging for those who wish to see a compromise in Northern Ireland. But the British government's lack of concern for the majority opinion in the province is also a rather worrying feature of the present situation.

For example, *Omnibus*, the official journal of the Northern Ireland Office Information Service, recently asked President Clinton this striking question: "The joint framework document has been launched, and the responses are broadly welcoming, how do you feel about it?" The posing of the question in this way amounts to a casual dismissal of the views, however ill-founded, of Northern Ireland's 13 unionist MPs. In his last two major interventions at the Dublin Forum – particularly on the vexed matter of the territorial claim – Mr Bruton has moved to meet some unionist concern. It is time the British government took a leaf from his book.

೮ ೮ ೮

CAN BLAIR'S PLAN AT LAST BRING PEACE?
The Times, 12 January 1998

T he denouement of the Northern Irish peace process is at hand. The recent revelation of the surprisingly unionist so-called "Blair plan" for the province has provoked a sharp reaction from the Irish government, the SDLP and, above all, Sinn Féin. Despite Dublin's apparent rejection of the Prime Minister's proposal, Mr David Trimble, the Ulster Unionist leader, remains a net beneficiary.

Mr Trimble now has an answer for his many critics within unionism (including four members of his own parliamentary party). He can tell them that this painful decision to stay within the talks process after the controversial admission of Sinn Féin in September – without, remember, even the realistic prospect of the decommissioning of a single IRA bullet – has been justified. The talks have not been the much-vaunted "political killing fields" for unionists.

By staying in, David Trimble has been able to intensify his dialogue with Mr Blair. In a recent interview, Trimble made it clear that he was comfortable with the language used by the Prime Minister in his May speech in Belfast – the key Blairite themes were the need for devolution in Northern Ireland and elsewhere in the UK and "sensible cross-border institutions". It is, however, even more valuable that he can say that he is comfortable with Mr Blair's current, more developed thinking about an Ulster settlement.

It is now clear that the British government supports a "Council of the Isles" body; this would link, on an east-west basis, the new assemblies in Scotland and Wales with Northern Ireland. When the Anglo-Irish framework document was published in 1995, easily the most substantive unionist criticisms focused on the weakness of the east-west section. This new proposed institutional east-west linkage is of enormous symbolic significance to unionists, who find it difficult to embrace a settlement based solely on a new north-south linkage on the island of Ireland. For Mr Trimble, there is the added advantage that the Council of the Isles is a traditional Ulster Unionist concept pioneered in the Molyneaux era, and some of those close to the leadership of Sir James Molyneaux have been among Mr Trimble's sharpest critics in recent months.

Although the Dublin government has reservations about the Council of the Isles formula, Bertie Ahern, the Taoiseach, has clearly not ruled it out at this stage. To go with the Council of the Isles concept and, indeed, to accept formally a new Northern Irish assembly, even one of an implicitly power-sharing sort, the Irish government and the SDLP need to have a fuller view of what Mr Trimble means by an enhanced programme of north-south co-operation. Mr Trimble needs to come up with a realistic proposal in this area.

Where does Sinn Féin fit into all this? Rather worryingly, at the moment Sinn Féin does not appear to be fitting in at all. Mr Blair will shortly try to mollify the republicans by announcing an apology for, and an independent inquiry into, the killing of 14 civil rights marchers in Londonderry's Bloody Sunday tragedy of January 1972, but there are worrying signs of instability within republicanism – signs which go far beyond the well-documented evidence of republican dissidence and resignations.

Since the start of the talks, Sinn Féin has continued to argue for an end to British jurisdiction in Ireland: even though it is the Irish government (not the British) which has publicly promised to drop its claim to jurisdiction in the event of an agreed settlement. That will inevitably leave Northern Ireland within the UK. Irish willingness on this score was again reiterated during Mr Trimble's important November meeting with Mr Ahern in London.

Sinn Féin remains opposed to the establishment of a Northern Irish assembly, even though that assembly was part of the Framework Document proposals which Gerry Adams claims, in other moods, to be his "bottom line". Mr Adams has also raised expectations of a mass release of prisoners by May – a rather unlikely development. Above all, Martin McGuinness has continued to insist that there could be a "fluidity" in the British position which would favour republicans.

The significance of the "Blair plan", even if it is never formally tabled in the talks, and represented only one approach that the Prime Minister was following sympathetically, is that it has knocked firmly on the head Sinn Féin's dreams of "rolling over" Mr Blair.

This moment, highly dangerous though it is, also gives Mr Trimble his opportunity. More important than the detail of any settlement, important though the detail is, is the settled will of the British state as embodied in the disposition of the man who is likely to be prime minister for some considerable time. There are, in Mr Blair's attitude, crucial implications for the working of a north-south body based genuinely on the principle of agreement and democratic accountability.

The Prime Minister has now given clear evidence of his disposition, and Mr Trimble can afford to gamble on the Prime Minister's good faith and take the risk – huge though it is – of rapidly shaping an understanding with those within the SDLP who are clearly in the market for a deal. The road from here leads either to relative stability – underpinned by the referendum choice of potential majorities of both unionists and nationalists – or to 25 more years of sectarian misery.

CB CB CB

Paul Bew

No Alternative to Talks
Irish Independent, 3 February 1998

This week the talks returned from Lancaster House to Stormont in a slightly anti-climactic and downbeat mood. It is all the more important, therefore, to point out that the joint papers – verbose and over-theoretical in places as they are – submitted by the two governments at Lancaster House, taken alongside the earlier Heads of Agreement, do permit us to outline a possible way forward.

This may seem to be a surprising claim. Some unionists – notably Jeffrey Donaldson in a celebrated moment of televised drama – have reacted angrily to the notion that the Framework Document is back on the agenda. The widespread perception is of nationalist and even republican claw-back, which may have destabilised unionists.

As Seamus Mallon drily commented on Donaldson's performance: "If we had paid him to do it, we could not have paid him enough". The point here, of course, is that the sight of Donaldson tearing up the Framework Document made it much easier for Sinn Féin to live with the allegedly pro-unionist Heads of Agreement document a fortnight before.

So much for spin and counter-spin. But it is important to stress some neglected underlying realities here. Both governments in London formally reiterated their positive attitude towards their joint co-productions, the Downing Street Declaration of 1993 and the Joint Framework Document of 1995. Nevertheless, circumstances have radically altered and thus have subverted, for good or ill, key parts of both documents.

The Downing Street Declaration is built around the notion that, following a permanent renunciation of violence, paramilitary groups could enter a talks process with other mainstream parties as to the way ahead. Permanence at the time was defined on the record by both governments as involving the prior handover of arms.

Does anyone think that this is the world in which we are now living in? Even the vaguest notion of permanence is now a pipe dream. The early discussion at Lancaster House was dominated by the open admission of one of the paramilitary groups, the UFF, that it had broken its ceasefire; others, still at the table, freely engage in threats of a return to violence at a later date. As for the joint framework, it, too, has suffered a similar buffeting at the hands of the historical process and the play of real interest. As various Dublin think tanks have long foreseen, the contradiction in Irish foreign policy between the strategy for the north and the strategy for Europe is now in full and rather exposed view. Ireland intends to join European monetary union on the first wave, while the UK has decided to delay entry for several years at least. What price then a project of all-Ireland harmonisation based on the growing integration of the two economies? This was, after all, very much the optimistic Dublin vision of how the Framework Document might actually operate in practice. For some years, this conception has been put on hold: and, if it does reappear, it will be at the behest of European rather than Irish pressures.

Another point is worth noting. The need for the "agreement of the parties", a cardinal principle of the framework – plus the compromises involved in preparing a package which might win a referendum in a society where 60 per cent of the voters are unionist – was always likely to lead to significant modifications of framework rhetoric.

In their east-west document, delivered at Lancaster House, the two governments again piously invoked the relevant paragraphs (39-49) of the Framework Document, but already within this limited quadrant, the Council of the Isles idea – not prefigured in the framework – has emerged as runner in the Heads of Agreement. This has, of course, only been possible as a result of another key change – the election of a Blair government with its commitment to devolution throughout the UK. From a unionist point of view, these developments have a clear implication. Individual areas of north-south co-operation can be approached on their merits without too much worry about anyone's grand design. Perhaps more important, devolution – once feared as a badge of difference or second-class citizenship – is now a projected norm throughout the UK. But from a nationalist point of view, there is also a clear advantage. As far as the SDLP is concerned, this time – unlike the Council of Ireland in 1974 – a new north-south body must start with significant functions, not a blank sheet. So long as the principle of democratic responsibility is accepted – as it already is by both governments – it ought to be possible now to produce a compromise acceptable to a majority in both major traditions. The main obstacle on the unionist side is a fear vigorously articulated by Robert McCartney of the UKUP and Peter Robinson of the DUP that cross-border co-operation, even that apparently focussed on low-key matters (animal health, fish health etc), is eventually intended gradually to strip away the British identity of the unionist community.

Mr McCartney, in particular, sets this in the context of British Labour support, until recently, of the policy of Irish unity by consent, but this is to ignore the iconoclasm of New Labour – Tony Blair now gives consent as the reason why there will not be Irish unity in his lifetime. The document on north-south co-operation, submitted by both governments at Lancaster House, is particularly revealing of this change.

In 1984, Labour's Ulster spokesperson, Clive Soley, advanced a programme specifically designed to bring about unity by consent through a policy of north-south harmonisation. But what about last week's document proposal for the harmonisation of social welfare? The message is banal and low-key: "action against welfare fraud" on a cross-border basis. As is typical of New Labour, this is hard-nosed and unsentimental, but it is also fundamentally rather more neutral in its political and constitutional implications.

At Lancaster House, Mr Blair's advice to the participants was to go straight from Heads of Agreement to detail. The implication is clear: some rather treacherous terrain should be bypassed. This does not seem to be an impossible task: indeed, if there is to be a settlement, this is the only likely route. The really profound obstacles to a settlement lie outside the talks forum itself.

Sinn Féin seems to be gaining at the expense of the SDLP, while many unionists regard the peace process as a fraud. There is a growing mood of inter-communal intolerance, and the desire for an outcome which humiliates, or at least stymies, the other side.

The decent impulses of some of the more sincere negotiators may well become irrelevant if this negative mood is allowed to get a firm grip on the mentality of both communities. All the more reason then for movement within the process; otherwise Northern Ireland faces another quarter century, perhaps not as violent, but every bit as dispiriting as the last.

ᘓ ᘓ ᘓ

A GOOD WEEK FOR THE ASSEMBLY
The Observer, 8 February 1998

It has been a relatively good week for the talks process. This was always likely – a lot of useful work on the northern assembly (Strand One matters) was effected during the Brooks-Mayhew talks in 1992.

All the parties except Sinn Féin are in a position to build on an implicit consensus. Now that SDLP leader John Hume has made it clear that an assembly is an essential part of his vision of accommodation, the question for Sinn Féin is: can it afford to break on this issue? On the one hand, by-election evidence suggests the party is still increasing in popularity. On the other, Mr Hume, backed by the Irish government, still has a powerful influence within the broader nationalist community in Northern Ireland. In alliance with Ulster unionists and the British government, they may well have the capacity to insist that the boundaries of any possible settlement include an assembly.

Nevertheless, the talks will fail if there is no parallel progress on north-south matters – an area that Ulster unionists still have great difficulty with. The papers published by the two governments at Lancaster House do, however, permit a more realistic appraisal of the possibilities. They reveal that a significant amount of cross-border co-operation is already occurring between the two governments. This is likely to continue, whether unionists agree to a settlement or not.

The greater integration between the two economies, a key intellectual prop of the Framework Document, now looks to be a rather more uncertain project. The decision by Ireland to join the single European currency, while the UK stays out, has seen to that. As the Lancaster House paper *North-South Co-Operation* reveals, it is difficult to talk, say, of harmonisation of financial services when the two countries will be inside different currency systems.

The papers also reveal the extent of the Labour Party's abandonment of "the Irish unity by consent" policy of the 1980s: as the Prime Minister told UK Unionist Party MP Bob McCartney at their recent meeting, the abandonment of this policy at the general election was significant. In the mid-1980s, Labour envisaged "harmonisation" of social welfare as involving the rerouting of Treasury welfare payments via a Dublin post office, so that northerners would get used to thinking favourably of the Irish government! Laughable in its way, the fact remains that such initiatives are a necessary part of any serious attempt to win Irish unity by consent.

It is now clear that any north-south body would be accountable to a northern assembly. The remit of such a body would initially be activities drawn from the less controversial elements set out in the *North-South Co-Operation* paper, but it is also clear that any expansion depends on the consent of the assembly. Michael Ancram, the minister responsible, said on the framework's publication: "The assembly, which by its nature is going to have a unionist majority, is always going to be in a position to say 'no, we won't do that'."

However, Sinn Féin leader Gerry Adams is right to say that the settlement envisaged by the two governments has an "all-Ireland" character. The concept reappears in the allegedly pro-unionist Head of Agreements. But what does this mean in practice? A significant influence on the Framework Document was an article by the late Dr John Whyte, Professor of Politics at Queen's University, Belfast. Dr Whyte drew attention to the large number of voluntary associations (151) which had an all-Ireland identity and in which unionists participated freely. He noted that the secretary of his local Unionist Association was also the secretary of one of these all-Ireland bodies. The implication is clear: north-south bodies are already a significant part of Northern Irish life, and they might have a role to play in any compromise. Fresh bodies worked, in effect, on the basis of the principle of consent.

Dr Whyte's article is a clue to the ethos underlying any settlement. There will not be Irish unity until the majority in the north support it. At the same time, an effort will be made to win northern nationalist acceptance of this reality by creating an Irish dimension as well as an equality programme. The union and unionism will survive, but it will be shifted on to a more liberal and flexible axis.

The Irish constitution and British legislation will also be amended to reflect the principle of consent. In this context, the Irish claim to jurisdiction will go; there will be no question of an Irish foreign minister reiterating continued Irish judicial sovereignty over the north, as Dick Spring did in the days following the Anglo-Irish Agreement in 1985.

ଓ ଓ ଓ

THE UNIONISTS HAVE WON,
THEY JUST DON'T KNOW IT

The Sunday Times, 17 May 1998

We are witnessing a desperate struggle for the soul of Ulster unionism. There are political careers at stake, to be sure; but so, too, is the whole political future of Northern Ireland.

Let us be clear – there is no possible confusion about the offer the British government is making to unionists in the referendum this week. This is why unionist rejectionists are so keen to muddy the waters. As one of them, Willie Thompson, the Ulster Unionist MP, says: "The more confusion there is, the more it will help the no camp".

So what is the underlying principle of the Stormont agreement? For five years, at least, Britain has been attempting to secure nationalist and republican acceptance of the legitimacy of British sovereignty in the north.

This agreement, which explicitly re-enacts that sovereignty, while at the same time securing the removal of the Irish Republic's territorial claim, marks the triumph of that policy. As one of the principal British negotiators dryly observed: "Do the unionists not see that this is about reconciling northern nationalists to British rule? Are they not interested in that?"

The Stormont agreement is not an ambiguous document. It has a carefully defined logic. The union of Great Britain and Northern Ireland is to continue for as long as it has majority support – and that, according to the prime minister, is likely to remain the case well beyond his own lifetime. There is, however, a price to be paid by unionists that includes the acceptance of power-sharing and cross-border co-operation.

Above all – and this is the really difficult part for them – unionists have to be willing to allow Sinn Féin a soft landing. After an IRA campaign of appalling violence, many unionists cannot yet find it in their hearts to do so, even though it means the collapse of the republican goal to bully and manipulate Ulster Protestants into a united Ireland.

The unionist majority is being asked to go a long way to meet the concerns of the nationalist minority. It does not necessarily follow that it is not in the interests of the unionists to do so.

However, while David Trimble's Ulster Unionists understand the nature of the agreement very well, it is clear that those unionists in the no campaign who reject its constitutional architecture do not even know what is going on. Republicans are more uneasily aware of the truth. As Mitchel McLaughlin has acknowledged: "The negative from the republican perspective is that it does, to an extent, legitimise the British state in Ireland".

Some of the unionists' anger is based on the narrowest "Little Ulsterism" – a stunning assumption that the union does not depend on opinion within the rest of the United Kingdom. It does not appear to matter to them that Mr Trimble has more credibility and respect in the House of Commons than any unionist leader since the start of the troubles, while his opponents have none. But it has to be admitted that others who have doubts include some of the most able thirty-something cadres of Ulster unionism. This group accepts that the agreement is sound enough, but it is alarmed by vagueness on decommissioning arms and the policy of early release of paramilitary murderers.

The prime minister is clearly doing everything possible to reassure these critics, and they will soon have to decide whether they can give him their trust.

So far, Tony Blair has been absolutely straight in his exposition of the fundamental principles of his Ulster policy. This is why he had the visible support in Belfast last week of Kate Hoey, the Ulster-born Labour MP who has always taken such a passionate interest in the affairs of the province.

This is not to deny that Mr Blair has brought pain to the Ulster unionists. From the start, the Blair government openly made a decision that it would not allow the issue of prisoners or decommissioning to stand in the way of an Ulster settlement. This was considered to be the great error of the Major government.

There is, however, the instructive irony here. Those unionists who are unhappy about Blair's radicalism on prisoners, for instance, tend to be largely the ones who prevented moves towards a deal during the first ceasefire in 1994, when it is quite clear that the Major government would have taken a very much more cautious line on this issue.

Equally clearly, however, Mr Blair has decided to abandon Old Labour's traditional flirtation with Irish nationalism and adopt, in effect, the Tory position – that Britain will not be a persuader for Irish unity, no matter how often Gerry Adams demands it.

There is, therefore, no reason for the present scale of unionist pessimism about the future. The republican movement has junked almost its entire belief system – everything from opposition to a Stormont assembly to its insistence on free-standing north-south bodies. Adams has one last card. He is relying now on unionists – enraged by carefully choreographed televised scenes of the Balcombe Street prisoners at his party conference – to tear up a settlement that secures the union.

Two weeks ago, the IRA issued a statement that there would be no decommissioning of arms. It is important not to take this at face value. When, for example, the Heads of Agreement document was issued by the British and Irish governments in January, the IRA issued a statement expressing extreme displeasure about its pro-unionist content. But everybody now knows that the Heads of Agreement contained the essential features of the Stormont agreement, which the republican movement has been compelled to support. The republican leadership knows that decommissioning is unavoidable, so long as the agreement sticks.

For Ian Paisley, the leader of the no campaign, this is a momentous week. His career has more than contributed to a marked decline in the credibility of Ulster unionism throughout the rest of the United Kingdom, but he has never been as close as he now is to delivering the killer blow. As republicans used to say wryly, it would be his final service to their movement.

If the no vote is large enough, unionism is condemned to more internal blood-letting and fragmentation. The agreement itself would then be stymied, but prisoners would still be released, and the IRA would definitely not hand in a single bullet.

Above all, a unionist block on the agreement is the only means by which Sinn Féin can regain the political initiative and reassert its traditional objectives.

If the unionists fail to vote yes to the Stormont compromise, they can be certain that they have forfeited their last real chance to shape their future.

 G3 G3 G3

INITIATIVE GOES TO TRIMBLE BUT HIS EDGE OVER UNIONIST OPPONENTS IS WORRYINGLY THIN
The Irish Times, 25 May 1998

It is important to say it now – it is not all over. David Trimble achieved a highly satisfactory result in Friday's northern referendum. He will be strengthened also by the massive determination in the Republic to drop the territorial claim.

With 71 per cent support, the Belfast Agreement has achieved a local legitimacy always denied to Sunningdale. It is said that when the then incoming British prime minister, Harold Wilson, saw the anti-Sunningdale unionists take a majority of the Northern Irish vote in the 1974 general election, he mentally wrote off the power-sharing executive. This is, indeed, in part the clue to the British government's apparent indecisiveness during the power-sharing executive's final crisis. This time the rejectionist force of unionism has not even managed to win a majority within unionism, let alone the people of Northern Ireland.

This fact alone gives the initiative to Mr Trimble. The men in the grey suits, referred to by dissident Ulster Unionist MP Willie Thompson, will not be coming for Mr Trimble this week.

Indeed, despite the loss of more than half his parliamentary party, Mr Trimble has retained the support of the great majority of the Ulster unionist electorate in the country. The most important of the No-voting MPs, Jeffrey Donaldson, has signalled that he has heard the voice of the Northern Irish people. Mr Trimble, therefore, has the initiative. But he also still faces significant problems.

Most seriously, the UMS/RTE exit polls, which got the result right, reveal an Ulster Unionist Party apparently becalmed at 19 per cent support, flanked on the one side by the Alliance at 9 per cent – which is perhaps suspiciously high – and the UK Unionist Party of Bob McCartney at 7 per cent. There is a sign here that Mr McCartney – for all that his own constituency appears to have supported a Yes vote – has a definite appeal to Ulster unionist voters who are disturbed by the agreement. The DUP retains a support level of 13 per cent. This places the total anti-agreement unionist party support at 20 per cent, while those unionist parties supporting the agreement are on 24 per cent – the PUP has 3 per cent, and the UDP 2 per cent. This is too close for comfort; the assembly's proper working is predicated on the unionist community electing a majority of representatives prepared to accept the spirit of the agreement. On present showing, Mr Trimble and his allies are likely to be able to do this, but it will be a closely fought contest, and nothing can be taken for granted.

Mr Trimble has other problems. A week from the end, the Yes campaign was on the verge of losing large segments of the Protestant middle class, which had initially reacted favourably to the agreement. The campaign was in serious difficulties, with a mediocre result in prospect.

The critical issue was the early release of paramilitary prisoners, in part, because it offended a public sense of morality but, in part, because it raised fears about the future. Was the day of the men of violence and the threats of violence really over? Here Mr Tony Blair's intervention was crucial. The Prime Minister's reassurances won back the Protestant middle class. However dreary it might be for Mr Blair, this group of conditional Yes people will continue to claim a lot of his attention before all this is over.

But the graphic fears on such issues are not Mr Trimble's only problem. More worryingly, the poll evidence suggests that a lot of unionists simply do not understand Mr Trimble's areas of negotiating success. They do not see the significance of the new British-Irish Council, designed to enhance linkages between the devolved assemblies of the UK. They do not still appreciate the importance of the removal of the territorial claim – after all, an acceptance by Irish nationalism of the legitimacy of British rule in the north. They do not see how he has achieved a model of cross-border co-operation which is non-threatening.

This is frustrating for Mr Trimble. Many observers feel he did a good job in the talks on such matters.

Mr Trimble has not exactly lost the argument on these points, but neither has he won it. In the next few weeks, he has to hope that the electorate is more reassured by his vision. He has a real chance of success – most unionists want any assembly to work properly, and they will be reluctant to return wreckers. But they can be provoked, and if their concerns are disrespected, they will do precisely that.

In the longer term, the future of Mr Trimble's unionism will depend on republicanism. One of the neglected clues to Mr Trimble's success is remoulding unionism lies in the assumption of some of his younger followers that they have nothing to fear from the arguments of Sinn Féin. Deprived of the historic grievance of partition and British rule by the voice of the Irish people in a referendum, what is it exactly Sinn Féin has to say when the arguments get tough?

There is still the "equality" agenda, but, it has to be said, fear of the equality agenda seems to have motivated very few unionist voters on Friday. If republicanism continues its current breakneck pace of revisionism, it can expect engagement with a more self-confident unionism very shortly.

Such an engagement is a necessary part of the "normalisation" of Sinn Féin, which must occur if Northern Ireland is to have stability. As Mr Trimble has long recognised, the principle of proportionality – also long accepted by the likes of Lord Molyneaux and Ian Paisley – means that Sinn Féin cannot be denied their own share of local pomp and circumstance. But for ordinary unionists to live with this, they have to feel that the threat of violence has gone for ever. But they also have to feel that Sinn Féin has lost the political initiative, in the sense of maintaining a relentless drive towards Irish unity. Only a direct and authoritative unionist engagement with Sinn Féin can provide that reassurance.

It is also necessary, of course, to remind people of the strength of the centre – Mr Trimble and John Hume together became a potent image in the last few days of the campaign. If people believe that there is a coherent common SDLP/Ulster Unionist Party programme of government, they are likely to rally to it.

03 03 03

TRIMBLE'S FUTURE ON THE LINE
WITH THE MARCHERS
Evening Standard, 6 July 1998

Why do we face yet another Drumcree? The fourth time around even the air of novelty has gone. The rest of the United Kingdom, mostly bored or horrified, watches uncomprehendingly the scene of confrontation – in fact, the rest of the UK is

watching a crisis which genuinely threatens the painfully constructed Stormont agreement on Ulster's future – the final act of a
drama which has deep roots in the history of Britain as well as
that of Ireland.

Ulster's Catholics expect Tony Blair to stop the Orange march
in Portadown this year as a proof of good faith, but if the government acts as they wish, it may destroy the unionist leader,
David Trimble, who is essential to the success of Mr Blair's Irish
policy.

Marching has been at the centre of the Northern Irish troubles
since they started in 1969. As a young civil rights supporter, I participated in a 70-mile march from Belfast to Derry, a route which
included many unsympathetic loyalist areas: this march was attacked at Burntollet Bridge at one of the great set-piece confronta-
tions of the early troubles. Civil rights activists paid little heed to
the wishes of local communities; like the Portadown Orangemen
today, we pleaded then the purity of our intentions. *We were
wrong* – like it or not, territoriality is part and parcel of Northern
Irish politics: in principle, it makes sense not to invade the space
of others without prior consultation.

There is a certain irony in the fact that the student marchers,
who were attacked at Burntollet, are regarded as heroes by the republican activists who want to stop the Orangemen walking down
the Garvaghy Road, even though the current republican position is
actually more akin to that of the loyalist protesters of 1969. In short,
no side in this conflict can claim any real moral consistency.

The consequence of that attack at Burntollet Bridge was a communal polarisation of emotion, which fatally undermined the re-
formist project of the then unionist Prime Minister Terence O'Neill;
will the Drumcree crisis have the same disastrous effect on Northern Ireland's newly elected First Minister, David Trimble?

Downing Street is frightened that it may be so. Bluntly, David
Trimble is more important to Tony Blair than Brendan McKenna,
the leader of the Portadown nationalists involved in this dispute.

That is why, despite the official ruling of the Parades Commission that the march should not go through, one of Mr Blair senior aides is reported to have asked for Mr McKenna to show some flexibility. For Mr Trimble this is an exceptionally difficult moment; it is perfectly obvious that he wishes, along with his newly effected nationalist deputy Seamus Mallon, to govern the province along the lines of inclusivity and fairness. But in 1995 Mr Trimble seized the leadership of unionism partly as a consequence of his support for the Orange revolt at Drumcree in that year. Mr Trimble's position is different today. In a recent interview he continued to praise the Orange Order's role in society, but noted that his own involvement in the Order was being greatly reduced as a result of his other responsibilities.

On Drumcree he seemed to acknowledge that the issue is not always a positive one, even with some unionist voters. Denis Watson, the leading Armagh Orangeman, tried but failed to gore Mr Trimble in last week's assembly election; others active in support of Drumcree have plastered Portadown with posters alleging that Mr Trimble is an MI5 agent.

Nevertheless, Mr Trimble cannot abandon the Orangemen. Most unionists in Northern Ireland – even key people in the pro-agreement camp – believe that there is no good reason to stop a church parade which has been going on since 1807. This year there is a new theme in Orange rhetoric: why should not (mostly) law-abiding Orangemen be offered a concession at a time when the government is signalling it is prepared to release IRA men from jail within two years? This line of argument cuts no ice with the beleaguered Catholic community in Portadown still mourning recent deaths at the hands of loyalist sectarian assassins.

Even though it is said that some of those with most influence on the Garvaghy Road are not fully loyal to his leadership, Mr Gerry Adams of Sinn Féin could help Mr Trimble out if he wanted. He could ask the residents to allow some type of limited procession. But why should Mr Adams wish to do so? His own voters strongly believe that Portadown Catholics are in the right anyway. If the British state faces down the Orangemen, it will exacerbate the divisions within unionism and make life hard, if not impossible, for Mr Trimble, who faces a leaking away of support over the summer months. This is Mr Adams' only route to a settlement more radical – and more satisfactory from his own point of view – than the one currently in place.

The government can only hope for the best. It can point out, at best, that half the Protestants in Northern Ireland support the Stormont agreement. In the past, sections of the Protestant community tacitly supported the Drumcree revolts because of the sense of powerlessness; today there is a unionist first minister in place, and many people want to see if he can deliver stability.

There are staunch Orangemen, too, who live in areas where Catholics are a majority, or who work with Catholics, who would prefer a quieter life. At least some of the Orange rhetoric promising a year of defiance comes from windbags who do not deserve to be taken seriously. The government may well calculate that the inevitable Orange reaction over the next few days will be relatively law-abiding – although there are already ominous signs that it may not be – and thus perhaps will not be too destabilising in its effects. But for things to fall out in any type of benign way, the government will require a very large measure of luck.

Mr Trimble, who this morning is reported as considering resignation, clearly believed that the system of direct rule, modified by riot or threat of riot, had to be replaced by something more stable; that is why he took so many risks to negotiate the Belfast Agreement. It will be tragic, indeed, if the last gasp of this old, unstable sectarian order should threaten the new and more tolerant order he is trying to bring into being.

CB CB CB

Paul Bew

AGREEMENT IS THE ONLY JUST WAY FORWARD
Irish Independent, 2 April 1999

I have been reading an interesting article by Hugh Logue. Mr Hugh Logue was recently appointed as part of the very able team which advises Seamus Mallon, Northern Ireland's Deputy First Minister Designate.

In his article, Mr Logue hails the agreement negotiated by the Northern Irish parties and the two governments. He notes that the SDLP ministers in the new power-sharing executive can be expected to promote the equality agenda in the north.

He sees the new North-South Council as a means of harmonising administration on an all-Ireland basis. He particularly applauds the appointment of the new Human Rights Commission. In Mr Logue's view, many people on both sides in the north saw the need for the agreement – only foolish action by the British government could make it fail.

Above all, Mr Logue sees the agreement as the beginning of British disengagement. He notes the paragraph in which the British government says it will support a united Ireland if a majority in the north so wish it. Such a commitment removes any possible basis for IRA violence and responds satisfactorily at last to demands made by Eamon de Valera on behalf of Irish nationalism. Mr Logue points out that an eminent unionist QC has grasped this unpalatable truth, despite the strangulated screams of those unionists who cannot face up to reality. Many nationalists instinctively warm to such an analysis – indeed, many unionists grimly feel in their hearts that it may be true. At this point, I should come clean. Mr Logue's article, which appeared in the *Irish Times* (17 January 1974), is over 25 years old. The agreement in question was the Sunningdale Agreement of 1973 – not for nothing did Seamus Mallon talk of the Good Friday Agreement of 1998 being Sunningdale for "slow learners". The language of the northern conflict is the language of endless repetition. The eminent QC in

38

question was Desmond Boal – though, of course, Bob McCartney specialises in very much the same sort of rhetoric nowadays. But the really interesting point is the failure of unionists to draw any comfort from the deficiencies of the Logue analysis; for good or for ill, unionists have had more ability to influence the political agenda and the behaviour of the British government over the last quarter of a century than Mr Logue had presumed.

Yet, it remains the case that unionists – to adapt Sartre's terminology – resemble more of a serialised group than a fused group. A serialised group is like a queue moodily waiting for a bus – united only in the hope that the bus will come and take them on to its destination, but with each member devoutly treasuring his or her own separate visions of the future.

Every unionist wants the same end – the union – but in most other respects there are different agendas at work. Nationalists, on the other hand, a more dynamic fused grouping, quite fail to be disconcerted by the weaknesses in the Logue analysis, seeing them if noticed at all, at worst, as delays in an inevitable process. There is all the optimism, not always justified of course, of the home crowd on the way to a football match. David Trimble has set his face against this defeatism in the unionist community, which he sees as an obstacle to the possibility of any decent settlement in the north. But he is in constant battle with the siren voices of a maudlin negativism, stressing the imminent British sell-out. Senator George Mitchell's new book, *Making Peace*, is very revealing on this point. Robert McCartney challenged Mitchell: will his report of 1996 really be independent of the government? Mitchell concludes that, on the whole, he did act independently.

He gives an account of a study meeting with John Major, which rather bears out his view, yet the irony is, of course, that Major was defending a pro-unionist position on prior decommissioning, while Mitchell was actually, at this point, convinced of the need for a compromise, a compromise which, on this point, the serious polls show this up: although it remains the case that one-third of the unionist community remains very strongly in favour of the deal.

There can be no doubting the fact that David Trimble is being asked to take a huge risk – 12 out of 13 unionist voters in the European election in 1999 preferred to support candidates who pledged "no guns, no government". Can anyone imagine Tony Blair, who responded so carefully to a much lower voltage message on the European elections in England, taking on and trying to buck the trend of public opinion this way?

In July David Trimble – though he was clearly conflicted – felt that he could not undertake such a task without the certainty of losing his leadership. His opponents within unionism – both inside and outside his party – hailed a great victory. His supporters heaved a sigh of relief, some of them hinting at a deal to be done in the autumn.

Over the summer, matters have, however, deteriorated: even more explicit evidence of IRA gun-running – in entire and complete defiance of the entire Good Friday Agreement – and involvement in murder (the tragic case of Charles Bennett) surfaced. The effect on unionist opinion has been predictably sour: where is the commitment to peace now?

In such a context, is it possible at all to set up a power-sharing government this autumn, including Sinn Féin and the unionists? The first thing to do is to respect the difficulty of the task. The Good Friday Agreement, and the subsequent referendum victory, were little short of a miracle.

But the unionists, too, have to come to terms with reality. For most of this decade, British and Irish policy has been diverted towards the inclusion of "the extremes" within the political process. The price originally demanded by both governments in 1993 – prior decommissioning of IRA arms – has been quietly dropped, but the objective remains the same.

year, David Trimble took the first step along this road. In his own words: "the UUP made a choice. When faced by either inclusivity or another generation scarred by self-defeating animosity, we chose inclusivity." A year on, it is not a bad moment to celebrate the fact that, at least, the effort was made.

 times times times

PEACE IN HIS TIME[2]
The Sunday Times, 4 April 1999

Senator George Mitchell is a hero of the Northern Irish peace process. The senior American politician gave up two years of his life (during which he was much troubled by his brother's death from cancer and fears about his wife's pregnancy on the other side of the Atlantic) to chair the multi-party talks on the future of Northern Ireland, which, for most of the time, seemed to be going nowhere. His book is a controlled, precise and, at times, evasive story of that process.

At one crucial moment in the week leading up to the agreement, Mitchell felt compelled to give an answer to a press question that was technically correct but less than completely honest. The fault lay more with the British and Irish governments, who were locked on the horns of a disagreement (which Mitchell did not wish to advertise), but it clearly troubles Mitchell, who draws attention to it here, although it barely registered at the time. The first reaction to this is to admire Mitchell's honesty and self-criticism. The second reaction is a more cynical one – why does he make so much of this relatively minor incident? His report in January 1996 declared a "clear commitment" on the part of paramilitary groups to decommission. In fact, Mitchell tells us that he

---

[2] *Making Peace* by George Mitchell was published by Heinemann in London in 1999 and by the University of California Press in 2001.

suspected the IRA was on the verge of returning to war, as it did with the Canary Wharf explosion a few days later.

The report appeared to mark the end of his involvement. Ambiguity, he makes clear, clouded the whole project. John Major had appointed an international commission, chaired by Mitchell, to deal with the dreaded problem, as yet unresolved, of IRA disarmament – a problem that loomed so large precisely because of the IRA's refusal to declare that their war was permanently over. Throughout 1995, unionists had refused to negotiate under such apparent duress. Mitchell's task was to provide a way round the impasse. His "resolution" was to advocate parallel decommissioning during talks rather than the British government's preferred option of prior decommissioning. Although Mitchell was told by many that his job had been to get the British off the hook of prior decommissioning, Major appears, in fact, to have been disconcerted when he realised Mitchell's intention. As a form of compensation for disappointed unionists, Mitchell agreed to include a provision for an election in the province – a particular demand of David Trimble's. It is clear from this account that Major's response to the report – accepting it and implementing the election provision – in no way constituted a "binning of Mitchell", as was so widely said at the time, and Mitchell would not have led the talks if this had been so.

Mitchell was in some ways a minimalist chairman – but that was his strength, as he concentrated on providing calmness at the centre of the storm. The most ruthless, unpredictable and effective figure here is Tony Blair. Mitchell makes it clear that Blair agreed a settlement document with Bertie Ahern over the final weekend of the talks and then when it became clear, as Mitchell felt was immediately obvious, that it would not wash with Trimble, Blair immediately launched a substantive renegotiation. Mitchell rightly praises Ahern's statesmanlike flexibility at this point – though the account of Ahern's actions and thought processes in the wake of his mother's funeral in Dublin can only be based on

Ahern's later account rather than Mitchell's direct observation. Mitchell's account – by stressing so much Ahern's inherent reasonableness – also underplays the intense pressure Blair placed him under at Stormont. As Mitchell makes clear, Ahern was forced to take the risk that, in his renewed efforts to meet Trimble, he might lose the SDLP, or rather more likely, Sinn Féin, from the process: in the end, Sinn Féin reserved its position on the agreement but remained in the process because of a radical programme of prisoner release.

Trimble also emerges as a serious figure. Always fearful that unionists would be blamed for the collapse of the peace process, he took a risk in accepting Mitchell as chairman of the talks, the naivety and/or cynicism of the Mitchell report having left a bad taste in many unionist mouths. Confronted with a Blair-Ahern document which did not contain the reassurances he believed he had gained from the prime minister only hours before, Trimble did not panic but successfully insisted on a significant restructuring of the text.

Mitchell argues – and the feeling is shared by many senior officials and, with hindsight, by some of the rejectionists themselves – that the Paisley-McCartney decision to withdraw from the talks after the second IRA ceasefire, and the rapid admission of Sinn Féin in the autumn of 1997, was their fatal political error, allowing Trimble the space to make a deal. *Making Peace* is a partial account of a process still insufficiently understood – and there will be later, fuller accounts. But, with this book, Mitchell has made a significant and decisive contribution to our understanding of the most serious attempt yet to achieve a historic compromise in Ireland, even if the process was a lot less Olympian and characterised by considerably more messy lowgradery and savagery than he allows.

ᕽ ᕽ ᕽ

WHY TRIMBLE HAS TO BE SUSTAINED IF THE PEACE PROCESS IS TO AVOID FAILURE

The Irish Times, 28 August 1999

The negotiation of the Belfast Agreement was nothing short of a miracle. Yet, somehow, during the past year, and despite great attention to detail – especially as far as Downing Street's role in the marching season went – neither the British nor the Irish government has quite fully internalised that fact.

The Blairists – so used to success elsewhere – have behaved rather like a beautiful girl who quite naturally, as is her due, received a ticket to the ball which did not have to be paid for.

The Irish government, on the other hand, self-confidence massively boosted by the continued success of the Celtic Tiger, has never really built on that self-confidence to make an analysis of the state of play within northern unionism free from those older, more cramped, ideologies rooted in the days when the mainstream nationalism of the Irish state was, in part, an ideology of compensation for relative material failure.

The two governments bear a share of responsibility for the current crisis of the peace process. They went for a quick fix last July which the local political marketplace simply could not sustain.

In the wake of the understandable row over Dr Mowlam's refusal to sanction the IRA in the wake of the Florida gun-running and the murder of Charles Bennett, the basic elements of intergovernmental strategy should be recalled, for the objective is to achieve settlement based, above all, on the inclusion of the extremists, the men of violence.

The governments believe that thus far they have saved hundreds of lives and are within an ace of tempting the republican movement into the lobster pot – to use a metaphor much used by officials – of safe, non-violent politics if only unionism would allow the setting up of an inclusive government in Northern Ireland as proposed under the agreement.

The generation now in office in London believes not only that heavy repressive measures like internment would not work against the IRA, but that any repressive measure is inherently fatally counter-productive – much better to co-opt the enemy. That is why prisoner releases have continued – in explicit defiance of a key section of the agreement.

As a young student in Cambridge in 1972, I remember well the protest demonstration which followed the tragic events of Bloody Sunday in Derry. I recall the personalities on that demonstration – they included people who are now key figures in New Labour.

The ethos of any political generation generally has its blind spots. Few of these people have a serious understanding of Ireland, but it is a political fact of importance, and it cannot be lightly ignored by the Ulster unionists, who have this week been disturbed by reports of the Patten Commission proposals on policing.

Throughout the year, Mr Patten has behaved as if he felt he had to please four main constituencies: Mr Trimble's pro-agreement unionist supporters; Mr John Hume's supporters in non-violent nationalism; the senior command of the RUC around Sir Ronnie Flanagan, the chief constable; Mr Adams and his followers in Sinn Féin and the IRA.

To please such incompatible groupings was always going to be difficult. If the leaked version of the report in the *Belfast Telegraph* is substantially accurate, Mr Patten will have satisfied John Hume's people above all; then Mr Gerry Adams; with the senior staff of the RUC less satisfied; while the pro-agreement Ulster unionist constituency of Mr Trimble – already under increasingly effective siege from a resurgent hardline Protestant politics – will be infuriated.

The change to the name and symbols of the force will be seen as an insult to the 300 policemen and women who died in the fight against both republican and loyalist terrorism. The localisation of the security structures as an open door to IRA influence and a Mafia state is an increasingly strong theme in public debate.

However, there is another way of looking at Mr Patten's apparently radical report. It removes the last remaining excuse for the maintenance of the IRA – every perceived grievance of nationalism will have been met or be in the process of being met.

There will not, it is true, be a united Ireland until a majority in the north vote for it – but that is what the people of Ireland voted for massively in the 1998 referendum. The British state in Ireland has thus been legitimised by the people of Ireland. In certain conceivable circumstances, radical IRA decommissioning could have been fudged; after Patten that is an impossibility.

Mr Blair simply has to deliver on his promise on the morning of the referendum in the *Irish News*: "Representatives of parties intimately linked to paramilitary groups can only be in a future Northern Ireland if it is clear that there will be no more violence and the threat of violence has gone. That doesn't just mean decommissioning, but all bombings, killings, beatings, and an end to targeting, recruiting and all the structures of terrorism."

After the IRA murder of Charles Bennett, and the Florida gunrunning, we are light years from that scenario, but as the prime minister said in the same article, there can be no fudge between democracy and terror. Earlier rather than later in the upcoming crisis, Mr Blair has to make a sober pitch to the unionist political class, allow it to mature in the public consciousness, and hope for the best.

In an interesting analysis of Irish politics in 1842, the Earl of Shrewsbury insisted that it was "fair to calculate ... that they who survive a long political struggle, may come out of it very different from what they were when they went in. They may have lost in prejudice and may have gained in experience".

He went on to insist that no serious politician could turn away from "the noble charge now entrusted ... of regenerating a whole people". In the 1840s these words fell on deaf ears with catastrophic consequences, but we have to hope as we enter this September that somehow this time the party leaders will find a way through.

Let us consider the consequences of failure to implement the agreement. The shrivelling of the Alliance party means that (outside the rarefied world of the PUP) nothing exists in the broad non-nationalist community to the left of David Trimble.

Mr Trimble has established a moral stature that was frankly inconceivable in the earlier years of his career. A British government which loses him will have to cope with the destabilising effects on Protestant politics for years.

Meanwhile, the SDLP will be destroyed by Sinn Féin as nationalist politics becomes increasingly embittered. Mr Adams will have no need or capacity to employ those more modernising or non-sectarian impulses which he sometimes appears to have.

These are the dangers – not some awful Plan B which the British government does not really appear to have in its back pocket. These dangers are dreadful enough to give us all food for thought.

 C3 C3 C3

THE LAST SHOT IS IN BLAIR'S LOCKER
The Politician – A Parliamentary Brief publication (Northern Ireland Special Edition), September 1999

This autumn the unionist political class in Northern Ireland will face a supreme test. How to admit Sinn Féin into the power-sharing government of Northern Ireland in the absence of prior decommissioning or, indeed, any other substantive sign from the IRA that the war is over. Ought it to be done? Can it be done? Why should an uncertain and doubtful unionist take the risk?

It is worth recalling that since at least the March meeting of the Ulster Unionist Council feeling within the broad movement of political unionism has tended to turn against the agreement. All the serious polls show this up: although it remains the case that one-third of the unionist community remains very strongly in favour of the deal.

There can be no doubting the fact that David Trimble is being asked to take a huge risk – 12 out of 13 unionist voters in the European election in 1999 preferred to support candidates who pledged "no guns, no government". Can anyone imagine Tony Blair, who responded so carefully to a much lower voltage message on the European elections in England, taking on and trying to buck the trend of public opinion this way?

In July David Trimble – though he was clearly conflicted – felt that he could not undertake such a task without the certainty of losing his leadership. His opponents within unionism – both inside and outside his party – hailed a great victory. His supporters heaved a sign of relief, some of them hinting at a deal to be done in the autumn.

Over the summer, matters have, however, deteriorated: even more explicit evidence of IRA gun-running – in entire and complete defiance of the entire Good Friday Agreement – and involvement in murder (the tragic case of Charles Bennett) surfaced. The effect on unionist opinion has been predictably sour: where is the commitment to peace now?

In such a context, is it possible at all to set up a power-sharing government this autumn, including Sinn Féin and the unionists? The first thing to do is to respect the difficulty of the task. The Good Friday Agreement, and the subsequent referendum victory, were little short of a miracle.

But the unionists, too, have to come to terms with reality. For most of this decade, British and Irish policy has been diverted towards the inclusion of "the extremes" within the political process. The price originally demanded by both governments in 1993 – prior decommissioning of IRA arms – has been quietly dropped, but the objective remains the same.

The fact is that the policy has been taken too far and with too much success to be dropped now. For most of the period since 1994, the IRA has been on a military ceasefire – hundreds of lives have been saved and, above all, the republicans and the unionists have agreed a historic compromise which preserves the union of Great Britain and Northern Ireland on the basis of consent – which is precisely the basis on which it has existed for the last 50 years since the post-war Labour governments' Irish legislation.

Those senior officials within both governments who had serious reservations about the policy are either marginalised or quite genuinely converted. This does not mean that everyone believes that the policy will succeed: quite a number believe that even if David Trimble does move, then the republican leadership has "quite a task of education" to ensure that their followers accept decommissioning.

There is also in key sectors of the British government a wariness about Irish government claims of republican good intent. But what unites everyone is the belief that, having come so far, the policy must be tested to the point of destruction. Anti-agreement unionism lives, however, in a completely different world. In a way that this is not understood properly outside Northern Ireland, it is underpinned by a strong religious sense. God, it is clear, would not approve of the early release of terrorist prisoners.

Can a compromise be morally distasteful but at some level operate to the advantage of the union? Impossible. Will the eventual – and still quite likely – victory of anti-agreement unionism massively weaken support for the union in the rest of the UK and thus bring a united Ireland not only closer but more likely on terms hugely disadvantageous to all?

Not a problem – if God so chooses to test the Christians of Ulster in this way, then so be it. There is an ambiguity – many of the anti-agreement electorate want a stronger unionist strategy than they perceive to be offered from David Trimble, but the people they are electing, to an increasing degree, reflect conservative, fundamentalist religious world views which are not hegemonic within Ulster unionist society – though they do animate significant constituencies.

More profoundly, the anti-agreement unionists have no strategy to defend the union. Indeed, this is the paradox; as Orangeism has declined as a force amongst elected unionist assembly members, religious and moral sentiment plays an ever more intense role within anti-agreement unionism.

Hence the wide appeal of a discourse which presents the agreement as morally corrupt. Hence also the reason why the Blair government's serious, hard-working and pragmatic efforts to reduce Orange Order alienation this summer will not have quite the political "pay off" the government hopes for.

How then can the agreement be saved? The first point is clear – the government can not afford to turn a blind eye to gun-running and murder. It has to say that it sees these things and notes how subversive they are of a genuine peace process. *The government has to respect the growing tide of anti-agreement scepticism and work with it, if it has to have any chance of modifying it.*

The point is simple: Mr Blair stands by all his pledges of clean government, free from the threat of violence and requiring IRA decommissioning as an act of good faith. If this is not done by a given date (May 2000), the whole experiment is over: remember Seamus Mallon's wise dictum that the political system could not withstand the pressure of an IRA failure to decommission by that date.

The fracas of the summer has, at least, dented conventional wisdom on one key point. Observers are beginning to acknowledge that a government could be set up which might last only a few weeks and then fall due to a failure to decommission. Indeed, even those who once argued that decommissioning could be viably ignored as an issue by a power-sharing government now accept that it will not be and can not be.

Previously it was felt that once admitted to government, Sinn Féin would be allowed to stay – whether they decommissioned or not. For the unionists the great advantage of moving ahead is clear. In its rhetoric and legislation, the British, also backed in terms by the US, appeared to be offering, in the event of a breakdown due to an IRA failure to decommission, direct rule with a green tinge, now made more acceptable by the repeal of the offensive sections of Dublin's articles 2 and 3.

For republicans and democratic nationalists this is the best and only chance to implement the agreement so strongly supported in their own community. At the moment the IRA hints menacingly at a new Canary Wharf, but while there is a chance of political development, to take such an action would seriously endanger progress for political expansion in the south.

But the key relationship is, as always, Trimble-Blair. This is the critical test. If David Trimble enters government on the basis of a post-dated resignation letter – designed to be actuated in the event of a failure to decommission – then Mr Blair has to say that he understands and supports this by legislative sanction. A few weeks of trial government – which ministers anyway must spend acquainting themselves with briefs and agendas long disused during the long era of direct rule – is in everyone's interest, above all because it gives Mr Adams his best shot at having the right conditions for decommissioning, and it allows the rest of us to see if he really can deliver.

The irony of all this is clear: to save the agreement, the British government must promise a decent, predictable form of direct rule in the event of the collapse of the power-sharing government – only then would unionists have the courage to jump and republicans the incentive to decommission. But where is the problem? This government has little interest in greener schemes like joint authority – direct rule is the only alternative to the agreement envisaged in the July election – it may as well make a virtue of necessity.

 CB CB CB

IRA CAN AFFORD TO PLAY BOTH SIDES OF ALLEY WITH IMPUNITY

The Irish Times, 27 September 1999

Does there lurk, somewhere in the IRA leadership, the last serious European revolutionary of the twentieth century? As the century peters out, there can be no question it has been dominated in Europe by the early success and then failure of radical revolutionary projects. The recent espionage revelations served at least to remind us how many people devoted their lives to such idealism.

But they are now curiously irrelevant – the epoch opened by the Russian revolution of 1917 closed decisively in 1989. But what an irony if dull old Belfast, of all places, turned out to be the last place on the continent where a spark of the old revolutionary zeal could still be found.

What is the evidence? Surely elements in the IRA leadership would not have contemplated such high-risk, high-cost activities as the Florida gun-running or various alleged assassinations, without being in possession of a coherent strategy which includes the serious option of a return to war? Against this, it has to be pointed out that the ceasefire now in place for most of the period since 1994 implied a serious awareness on the part of the collective leadership of republicanism of the limits of the old military campaign.

Above all, republican leaders at this point do not have to make a definitive choice – as they are so often urged to do by unionists – between democracy and terror. The various provocations – the Florida gun-running being the most stark – could be part of a serious renewal of a revolutionary strategy, or they could simply be "part of a strategy of tension" within the peace process, designed to make it harder for unionists to work the Good Friday Agreement and thus earn the odium for its collapse.

If, as an increasing number of serious observers – including some traditionally hostile to this notion – claim, the republican movement is ceasing to be a monolith, it can, nonetheless, afford to play both sides of the street with impunity. The prospect of a unionism shorn of its historical triumphs in the negotiation of the agreement – the return of the Stormont assembly, the acceptance by the Irish people of Northern Ireland's legitimacy within the UK – led by, say, Jeffrey Donaldson, who is unlikely ever to get a friendly hearing from the British Prime Minister, Tony Blair, can only have republicans licking their lips in anticipation.

The cruel reality for pro-agreement unionists is ineluctable. Only in the period after the establishment of the executive will the republican movement be forced to make the hard decision to take the radical action of substantive decommissioning or collapse the executive by failure to do so and thus earn the increasingly well-advertised scorn of the British government, which has the power – and little incentive to do otherwise – to suspend anti-unionist initiatives *sine die*. The peace process will then have been driven to the point of self-destruction by republican inflexibility.

Intellectually, these points are widely understood within unionism, but emotionally and morally, the balance of forces still does not favour any radical move by David Trimble to break the deadlock.

The Patten Commission report – with its naively heavily-advertised dependence on sources which did not support the making of the agreement when it mattered – may have done for Mr Trimble. Mr Patten's claim that somehow Mr Trimble should have known the precise outcome was implicit in the Good Friday Agreement ignores the history of the discussion of the issue in the last weeks of the talks and, indeed, in the days leading up to the appointment of the commission.

More substantively, Mr Trimble knows that the badge, say, of the RUC is not a republican badge, but then the agreement, as republicans always tell us, is not a republican agreement. It would have been far better if Mr Patten had said that his hard choices were dictated solely by the need to win more nationalist support for the new police service.

Mr Trimble has not been helped by the SDLP. Had he responded to the SDLP's call to resign as first minister, the peace process would already be dead, because it is most unlikely that Mr Trimble can find again the unionist votes necessary to be reelected.

The broad nationalist middle-class SDLP constituency is in a sorry state. It has come to resemble in an uncanny way intellectually inert pre-Troubles middle-class unionism: a slightly pompous establishment, sharp-tongued and dismissive of the legitimate concerns of others and, above all, unable to grasp that the day when the British state dropped good things into the collective maw has just, with the delivery of the Patten report, passed away for good.

Angered by its recent marginalisation in the peace process, dismayed by the seemingly irreversible electoral rise of Sinn Féin, the SDLP is now hopelessly dependent – irony of ironies – on the much-maligned David Trimble to save it from itself by setting up an executive which would be the party's last chance to retain hegemony within northern nationalism.

Given all this, David Trimble must be sorely tempted to walk away from the whole mess. But he cannot do so for the simple reason that he is the last remaining hope for stability in Northern Ireland and, by logical extension, the island of Ireland as a whole.

Admittedly, his survival does not guarantee stability – Irish nationalism may simply not be able to accept the boundaries of the agreement – but his failure guarantees long-term instability and communal recrimination.

One fact is crucial: the forms of disunity with unionism are totally dysfunctional – a Paisley vote has long since ceased to be an insurance policy which deters the British government – while the forms of disunity within nationalism and republicanism have served to increase nationalist leverage over the system.

If the agreement survives, Mr Trimble has a shot at establishing unionist unity around a modernising programme as DUP ministers serve alongside his own. Mr Trimble's critics insist he should have done more during the year to defend the RUC or influence the government's agenda in other "reserved" areas. They may have a point – but surely, the bigger question is this: how does a political community which is still a substantial majority manage so consistently to punch below its weight, and is there any chance of this changing – and change would also be to the long-term benefit of nationalist Ireland – in the absence of the full implementation of the agreement?

 Cß Cß Cß

GRUMBLING "GREY VOTERS" PUT THE PARTIES IN A SPIN

Sunday Business, 17 October 1999

In May 1949, Peter Mandelson's grandfather, Herbert Morrison, told the House of Commons: "Quite frankly, this government is not going to seek and take the initiative for the purpose of losing a part of the UK. If Irishmen get together and make agreements among themselves, that is a situation which we will consider. But it is no part of the business of this government – and it is not going to do it – to take the initiative to diminish the territory of the UK."

What is striking about Morrison's position is its modernity. The Labour cabinet had been advised that Ireland's war-time neutrality meant Britain would never have an interest – even if a majority in Northern Ireland supported it – in bringing about Irish unity. The then home secretary rejected this advice and formulated the modern doctrine of consent to define Northern Ireland's place in the UK.

In the mid-1950s, R A Butler moved the Tories back towards a more traditional position, asserting, privately at least, the importance of Britain's strategic interest in Northern Ireland. But it was the Morrison doctrine, embodied in legislation, that defined Northern Ireland's status.

In short, Morrison was no closet British imperialist but a formulator of a reasoned democratic position on the Irish problem that clearly anticipates the 1993 Downing Street Declaration – strongly supported at the time by his grandson – which claims that, while Britain will not be a persuader for Irish unity, it has no selfish economic or strategic interest in Ireland.

Many close to David Trimble are pleased at Mandelson's appointment as Northern Ireland Secretary because of his style and efficiency as a politician. He and Trimble share a common crispness, not to say briskness of mode.

Up to the signing of the Good Friday Agreement last year, the division of Labour – Mo Mowlam catering to national sentiment, while Tony Blair smoothed ruffled unionist feathers – worked effectively, but has since failed to deliver. Blair cannot possibly deal effectively with all the detail, and when he was distracted, as with Kosovo, Trimble lost the ability to influence, and his disillusioned supporters asked – what use is this agreement?

We now need clear lines of efficiency and responsibility in the government. The Mitchell talks are bogged down, and it does not yet appear that the republicans will make a credible offer to decommission within weeks of the setting-up of an executive.

If they maintain this stance, the only way towards implementing the agreement involves a revival of a modified form of Blair's summer plan, whereby republicans either decommission or face the suspension and review of the agreement. This time the details must be worked out more clearly. Mandelson is the sort of politician who can get it right, but a lot depends on the general atmosphere within the community.

His first major act in office – to visit a centre helping the victims of violence – was not on Mowlam's schedule. It showed the glimmering of a new governmental recognition of reality: only 5 per cent of the victims of the troubles fell at the hands of state forces, and these mostly in uncontroversial circumstances.

The state cannot afford to mimic the self-absorbed, self-admiring and capriciously cruel culture of the paramilitaries, who, in the republican case, inflicted huge suffering for a now abandoned cause – forcible coercion of Protestants into a united Ireland.

It is essential to get to the truth of those cases with serious question marks about the behaviour of soldiers and police officers. I am a historical adviser to the Bloody Sunday tribunal, which is making strenuous efforts in this regard.

Nevertheless, the media focus on this and similar inquiries has created a decided impact on mainstream public opinion. It seems – quite wrongly – that the state is privileging a small number of deaths and forgetting the thousands that are the responsibility of paramilitaries, whether loyalist or, more frequently, republican.

Unionists who voted for the Good Friday Agreement did so to put the culture of recrimination behind them, even if it meant tacitly accepting that the historical record of their own leadership had been at best unimaginative and unimpressive.

Blair's great skill in the referendum campaign was to convince them that the future would not be dominated by the past. The history of the last year has (through no intention of Mowlam and her advisers) raised doubts on that, but nobody is more capable of directly addressing them than Mandelson. Some frank and open discussion of these issues would go a long way.

Such discussion can only lead to a painful conclusion for the republicans. A movement that once signalled that it would be criminal to inflict misery on society for anything less than the full republican ideal, has now – quite rightly and within its terms – bravely come to terms with the reality of its inattainability.

In that sense, but in that sense only, there has been a seismic shift. The public debate must keep this point in focus, otherwise the Ulster unionists and the SDLP – the parties that gave us the Good Friday Agreement while Sinn Féin reserved its position – will lose out to a perception that Sinn Féin owns and directs the dynamic of the agreement.

This, in essence, was the tactical error of the period since the Good Friday Agreement. Ministers and officials, while in no way personally accepting the Sinn Féin version of reality that the agreement is inherently part of a transition to Irish unity and that inquiries such as Bloody Sunday or Chris Patten on the RUC are down-payments of British guilt, designed to smooth the past. It has seemed better to collude in the republican version of reality – most notably on the continued release of prisoners while gun-running went on – than risk a Provo return to war.

No minister dared repeat Blair's 1997 claim that the doctrine of consent meant that there would not be Irish unity in his lifetime. Such prudence may even have been justifiable, but now three things are clear.

The Adams leadership is firmly in control of the republican movement, and the pressing security threat comes from those who have already split off in counties such as Armagh and, more surprisingly, Derry. Second, his leadership has no stomach for a return to war. Third, it is stronger within its own community than the Trimble leadership, which needs the government to start telling the truth about the Good Friday Agreement. This, Mandelson might like to recall, is where grandfather Morrison has a lot to tell us.

Otherwise we are in the grip of a classic tragedy: everyone knows what they ought to do to save the process but can not bring themselves to do it. Most unionists still loathe Sinn Féin, but they know life has to move on.

Most nationalists know that an IRA refusal to decommission while Sinn Féin ministers sit in government opens up a ghastly vista of a new type of state terrorism. Mandelson has to create the mood whereby people feel confident enough to act on their own best impulses.

CB CB CB

HOW TRIMBLE CAN BREAK THE IRA ARMS LOGJAM
Sunday Independent, 14 November 1999

David Trimble has a nice line about the Good Friday Agreement – used to much good effect last week in Washington in the White House, the Nixon Centre and the Georgetown dinner tables. He is prepared to take risks for the agreement, he says, but not with the agreement. It is a nice line, but it does not describe the perilous situation he is now in. The truth is that David Trimble now may only be able to save the agreement by taking risks with the agreement.

The defining feature of the current conjuncture is clear enough. The IRA, in minimalist mode, is not offering – and is not likely to offer – the necessary assurance that will convince the bulk of the Ulster Unionist Party that decommissioning is definitely going to happen, even if Mr Trimble first takes the risk of establishing a power-sharing government in Northern Ireland. Mr Trimble's increasingly confident band of internal unionist critics believe they will be able to expose the unionist leader's previous pledges on this issue as hollow.

In fact, Mr Trimble's relatively flexible interpretation of the unbreakable "no guns, no government" principle has been tolerably consistent for some considerable time, but the problem goes deeper. Quite simply, Northern Irish society cannot sustain this agreement if this agenda of the agreement *appears* to be set by the IRA leadership.

I say "appears" because in many respects this is a fantastic illusion. Late on the Thursday before Good Friday, key Sinn Féin people at the talks did not really grasp the fact that the SDLP and the Ulster Unionist Party had constructed a centrist deal which marginalised the republican project.

David Trimble is painfully aware of the fact that only the implementation will see the outworking of the negotiating triumph – a working Northern Irish assembly, pragmatic north-south and east-west institutions, and the formal end of the irredentist ideology of the Irish Republic. Ironically, the focus on decommissioning has allowed Sinn Féin to give the entirely spurious impression that it is *their* agreement which the Ulster unionists, fearing the worst from its operation, are doing everything possible to halt in its tracks.

Nevertheless, in one important respect, we have all been dancing to a tune set by the IRA leadership. They hinted at the possibility of decommissioning during the talks; they denied it in the end. They hinted at the possibility of decommissioning after the negotiation of an agreement; they denied it in the end. They hint now at the possibility of decommissioning after the executive is established; will they not deny that in the end? After all, they have succeeded in doing what John Hume as well as the British and Irish governments, let alone the unionists, said they could not do – negotiate with guns under the table. In this sense – and in this sense only – the IRA leadership is driving the process.

This is where the more percipient critics of the process – like *The Daily Telegraph* or Conor Cruise O'Brien – draw their strength. Listening to Dr O'Brien's eloquent address to the Irish Association in Carrickfergus this weekend, I was struck by the Burkean consistency of his argument. This is hardly surprising, because Dr O'Brien is the greatest biographer of Edmund Burke, by far the most influential Irish political thinker. Burke saw extremist French revolutionaries as "a species of men, to whom a state of order would become a sentence of obscurity"; he could not believe that such men would voluntarily switch off "the disorders which are the parents of all their consequence". Dr O'Brien believes the same thing about the IRA.

Mr Trimble has an answer to all this. It is the peculiar genius of the agreement that the republican political class does not face a "sentence of obscurity" – even if their foot-soldiers do, hence their hostility to decommissioning – but rather than look forward to office and all the other fruits of modern celebrity. Increasingly, Mr Trimble believes they have bought into that. Mr Trimble, too, is a Burkean, as his Nobel speech in Oslo revealed clearly. Precisely 200 years ago, as today, Burke's legacy divided Irish unionism. As Dr O'Brien has pointed out, more brilliantly than anyone else, Burke, a man with strong Irish Catholic family associations, believed that the success of the union was dependent upon Catholic emancipation. Burke's critics – notably Patrick Duigenan, the partisan Protestant pro-union MP for Armagh – disputed this; Catholics, in this view, were entitled to equality in "civil privileges", but they must be excluded – because of their fundamental disloyalism – from any role in government. In declaring so emphatically for Burke as he did in Oslo, David Trimble was attempting to effect a closure in a debate which has raged for two centuries within Irish unionism. He was openly acknowledging that civil equality is not enough; Catholics must be included within government if the union is to be sustained and the closest possible connection between Britain and Ireland maintained, exactly as Burke desired.

Mr Trimble believes that any nationalist or republican who, accepting the principle of consent, becomes part of the governmental structures within the UK state, is – whatever the genuinely held long-term aspiration – structurally a unionist. But the republicans make it clear to anyone who will listen to them in Belfast that they do not accept the principle of consent. That will not matter, as the institutions and ethos of this agreement close in around them, or so Mr Trimble reasons. But here lies the rub ...

Mr Trimble believes in this agreement. He is immersed in its minutiae, lovingly handcrafted by himself. The republicans see his vulnerability and squeeze him ruthlessly in the decommissioning negotiations. He genuinely does not want to take a risk with this agreement, *his* agreement, but he is going to have to do so, for this reason: above all, an agreement which functions without decommissioning is stripped of its ethos – the democratic principle – for in this situation the recalcitrant element in the IRA leadership would be determining an outcome against the preferred option of the overwhelming mass of the Northern Irish people, including a substantial slice of Sinn Féin voters. In some ways, it would be a hollow republican victory – merely allowing the maintenance of self-deceiving and self-destructive illusions in militant heartlands – but it would sour the process for the rest of society, which needs to believe that a line in the sand has been drawn and that the era of threat is over. In short, the agreement without decommissioning would lose its moral authority. The question of timing is entirely a secondary and tactical issue, though one of great importance.

Mr Trimble now has one way out. Senator Mitchell's deal does not guarantee that the functioning of the agreement depends on decommissioning – but Mr Trimble can, by the device of a post-dated resignation letter, to be activated in the event of a republican failure rapidly to meet their obligation to decommission after the setting-up of the executive. President Clinton has said that Mr Trimble has every right to walk away at such a point; the British and Irish governments can hardly disagree.

Mr Trimble may not like it – he is deeply committed to this agreement, as a good deal for unionism and the people of Northern Ireland generally – but the harsh fact remains that he is going to have to take risks with the agreement to have even a decent chance of saving it.

ख ख ख

TRIMBLE SEEKS TO COMPLETE ULSTER JIGSAW
The Times, 20 November 1999

O nce he stood for "not an inch", now he has placed himself out on a limb. This weekend David Trimble seems remarkably serene, but he knows he has travelled well in advance of where his Ulster Unionist Party is happy to rest. Can he use the days ahead to persuade Northern Ireland's biggest party to make its greatest leap of faith yet? Will he be allowed to enter government with Sinn Féin before the IRA have decommissioned their weapons?

Eyes will be focused on the unionists this week as they prepare for the party meeting that will decide the matter. For dissidents and sceptics within the UUP there is one question: why did their leader find it possible to do a deal in November when he could not do one in July?

Mr Trimble has given us his stated reasons. This time the republican leadership is committing itself – rather than having its position interpreted, possibly over-optimistically, by the British and Irish governments. Instead of having to accept Tony Blair's conviction that there was a "seismic shift" in the IRA's attitude to decommissioning, Mr Trimble has had the chance to test Gerry Adams' good faith during George Mitchell's 11-week review of the peace process.

The role of Senator Mitchell in bringing the two sides together has been integral. Mr Mitchell developed a talent for tedium in the Senate, a capacity to hear out filibusters, debating points and amendments. It meant that he could allow protagonists to get everything off their chests, the better to open their minds.

That ability allowed him to hear out each side without exhausting his own patience. When republicans and unionists met to discuss the governments' "way forward" document in July, both sides felt pressurised by aggressive spin and imposed deadlines.

The review this autumn proceeded at a much more considered pace. Not only did Mr Mitchell allow the protagonists to outline their positions in full, he encouraged them to fraternise outside those trenches. By insisting that the parties share meals with him, with no discussion of politics allowed, a rapport was established. Over fast food in the US Ambassador's residence, he turned the conversation to fly-fishing and reeled in his catch.

The process culminated this week in a series of choreographed statements. The careful sequencing bore the hallmark of Peter Mandelson's delicate touch. The Secretary of State ensured that no toes were trodden on as each party's prima donna took his turn.

In the elaborated ponderous tones of the documents, there was no pandering to the media appetite for drama. They were reminiscent of the "stately Vergilian numbers" with which William Pitt introduced the union of Britain and Ireland 200 years ago. But, in the detail, Mr Mitchell and Mr Mandelson hope there will be a casting out of devils. They can point to evidence of a shift by the republicans.

Since the Good Friday Agreement, republicans have always insisted that the guns are silent and that this is all they have to deliver within its terms. Their stance on decommissioning has been "no, nothing, never", coupled with a highly dubious claim that all the other key parties understood this in April 1998. They refused to engage with the notion that the Belfast Agreement's explicit reference to a politics free from the threat of force was incompatible with a refusal to decommission.

Now, in a series of agreed statements, General de Chastelain's International Commission on Decommissioning has linked the need to decommission paramilitary weapons to the issue of latent threat: the republicans (including explicitly the IRA) have now themselves spoken out against latent threats for the first time.

Nevertheless, Mr Trimble's project now faces severe difficulty. In July, Sinn Féin briefed both its members and the press that the so-called seismic shift on decommissioning alleged by Mr Blair was all a "con". This time around, Sinn Féin leaders appear to have behaved with discretion and honesty in their dealings – a discretion that was praised by Mr Trimble in Washington recently. But inevitably – and it will be no surprise to Mr Trimble – some of last summer's offenders are now beginning to show recidivist tendencies.

One senior republican, Martin Ferris, alleged on Tuesday that no decommissioning would take place, telling US supporters: "If IRA guns are silent, the executive is up and doing business, the assembly is up and doing business, why on earth would Blair collapse all of that over the non-decommissioning of guns that are silent anyway?" Mr Ferris spoke before the announcement that the IRA would appoint an interlocutor on decommissioning and has subsequently been reported to have rowed back.

But Mr Ferris has not been alone in casting doubt on the credibility of future decommissioning. Pat Doherty, Sinn Féin's vice-president, has also been reported in America as rubbishing the prospect of any arms hand-over. His opposition to decommissioning in the past has given unionists cause for concern.

Once the unionists are in government with Sinn Féin, will anyone dare to bring the show down? At this point, Mr Trimble's last unstated reason for doing the deal comes into play. For a long time, Mr Trimble has wanted a Secretary of State for Northern Ireland who could act as his effective partner in implementing the agreement; in Mr Mandelson, he hopes he has one.

We need to hear soon from Mr Mandelson how London will react to republican failure – for whatever reason – to live up to its side of the bargain; the comments of Mr Ferris and Mr Doherty have made urgency imperative in this matter. If ever there was a chance for an uncomplicated positive sell of this new deal, it has now evaporated.

It may well be that Mr Adams and Martin McGuinness, having given the impression that they are moving on the arms issue, will be extremely reluctant to default on that understanding. The standing and prospects of Sinn Féin in the republic are dependent on building their party's credibility through the peace process.

Nevertheless, the undecided and worried delegates of the Ulster Unionist Council – who will decide this issue a week today – will want to know how they are placed if a republican grassroots revolt prevents decommissioning.

Vulnerability is the condition of all achievements, wrote the Marxist Terry Eagleton in his book *New Left Church*, published in the radical 1960s. He can hardly have expected that, as the 1990s came to a close, the Ulster Unionist leader of that still conservative party would provide such startling evidence of this principle.

It is a dramatic shift: but Mr Trimble's more prosaic delegates, many from small town and rural Ulster, will want to hear something about the insurance policy if it all goes wrong. Before they move an inch, they will want to know that they will not be left out on a limb by the government.

CB CB CB

A NARROW MARGIN OF REAL HOPE
Sunday Mirror, 28 November 1999

David Trimble put his leadership of Ulster unionism on the line yesterday in order to save the peace process. He succeeded – by the narrowest effective political margin. No more will republicans be able to say they are unjustly being excluded from the government in Northern Ireland.

Next week, the new power-sharing cabinet will be formed, bringing Paisleyites and Sinn Féiners together in a new administration for the first time ever. It is a startling development, one which, if sustained, makes a return to war in Northern Ireland inconceivable.

For New Labour, this is a moment for reflection. It has shown itself as having come fully to terms with the principle of consent since taking power in 1997. This means Northern Ireland will not leave the UK unless a majority in Northern Ireland support that.

This is the clue to Tony Blair's success. But New Labour has not yet come to terms with the unionist people of Northern Ireland. Many New Labour members still do not grasp the magnitude of David Trimble's achievement in modernising unionism.

They unconsciously tend to think that IRA violence has been in some way justified by the rigidity of the Ulster unionist mentality. After yesterday's dramatic vote, even the dullest mind must question if this is really true. Let us be clear about the enormous significance of what is happening under our noses.

Nigel Dodds, of the Paisleyite DUP, will next week be expected to join a cabinet alongside representatives of the same republican movement which three years ago opened fire on him and his police guard, when he was visiting his very sick child in hospital.

It would have been impressive in the past week if someone in government had shown that this is asking rather a lot of any human being – even if it is what 71 per cent of the people of Northern Ireland in a referendum wanted to happen. We are on the verge of the greatest breakthrough yet in the peace process – it ought to be approached with a little moral seriousness.

The government could have increased. Mr Trimble's majority yesterday by a number of steps, which were not taken for fear of making life difficult for Gerry Adams. They could have reaffirmed in broad terms Tony Blair's commitment that he valued the union. They could have dealt with the issue – a burning one for many unionists – that the government is casually breaking its pledges on decommissioning and punishment beatings. The failure to do these things pushed Mr Trimble into a corner.

Apparently losing the debate within his own party, he made the decision to employ the tactic of post-dated letters of resignation to show he really would walk away from the power-sharing government if there is no decommissioning of IRA weapons in the next few weeks. As Mr Adams made clear yesterday, this new unionist strategy gives him some cause for concern.

But, these cavils apart, nobody can take away from Mr Mandelson's stunning achievement. He played a major role in winning back Mr Trimble's deputy leader John Taylor. The award of the George Cross to the RUC was a brilliant move. Peter Mandelson has carried himself with dignity in a way which has impressed a sceptical populace.

Mr Mandelson's many critics in the UK will have to come to terms with the fact that his record thus far in Northern Ireland has been highly impressive and that he has been able to make the difference between success and failure. His colder, more precise, less emotional style was exactly what the peace process needed at this point.

So what happens now?

The Good Friday Agreement will at last be implemented – a genuine cross-community government will be established next week. Then the waiting begins – will the IRA actually decommission its weapons?

Mr Adams was anxious yesterday to remind us that he has given no definite promise to bring about disarmament. He is quite right. But he has heavily implied that, if David Trimble moves first to set up a government, he would reciprocate. An act of perceived bad faith now would be a public relations disaster.

Far better for Mr Adams to move quickly to exploit the honeymoon period of the new government and make a decent gesture on arms – but hardliners in the IRA will do everything possible to stop him and they might succeed.

If they do, the agreement will again enter crisis, because the Ulster Unionists may be forced by opinion within their own party and community to withdraw from the deal. If that happens, we are all back in the mess.

But let us hope that the opportunity given by the new millennium will be seized to create a lasting peace in Ireland.

03 03 03

THE INSTITUTIONS OF THE GOOD FRIDAY AGREEMENT ARE IN TATTERS BUT ITS PRINCIPLES ARE INTACT

The Independent, 13 February 2000

In November, David Trimble was forced, with the greatest reluctance, to take a risk with the Good Friday Agreement in order to give it an extra phase of life. He set up the power-sharing executive in Northern Ireland without any IRA decommissioning. Last week Peter Mandelson, with equal reluctance, was forced to put the executive on hold. Mr Mandelson suspended the institutions of the agreement in order to maintain its prospects and principles. Mr Mandelson, in other words, took a risk with the agreement in order to save it.

The alternative was to desert Trimble, who would have forced the suspension by resigning anyway. Such inaction would have vindicated his many right-wing unionist enemies who claimed that the British government would always cave in to the threat of IRA violence in a crisis. To their credit, Mr Blair and Mr Mandelson stuck to their bargain with Mr Trimble. The White House pressed Mr Blair not to suspend right up to the end. Mr Blair has preserved Mr Trimble's capacity to do good in the province; just as important, he has renewed his own capacity to do good.

The Irish government, on the other hand, has misread British intentions over the past fortnight; this crisis apart, some of its officials have seemed ill at ease with the new post-agreement dispensation and its implications. The new dispensation requires an examination of many of the traditional anti-British themes in Irish public life. A greater civic unity and a better east-west relationship require such examination. This is a point that has been strongly made by Sir David Goodall, the Cabinet Office official who played such a key role in the Anglo-Irish Agreement of 1985, which first gave Dublin great importance in Northern Irish affairs.

Why did the Irish Ambassador to the UK, Ted Barrington, never pay a formal visit to Mr Trimble, marking the new openness? It is possible to feel great sympathy for senior Irish officials spending sleepless nights negotiating with the Sinn Féin leadership and clutching at straws in an effort to avoid last week's denouement. But the fact remains that these same officials promised to stand by Mr Trimble last year if he jumped, and there was no IRA reciprocation on the arms issue. In fact, there was little sign of any real solidarity with Trimble last week, and even absurd speculation in senior republican and nationalist sources about the possibility of an alternative pro-agreement unionist leadership emerging.

In a rather blatant effort in which a PR battle, which was being lost in such crucial theatres as the US media, the IRA offered some new language to General de Chastelain, and he has responded with a more optimistic though decidedly ambiguous report. The IRA's real intentions on the arms issue are still unclear. The key issue is what might be called "the Keenan doctrine", in deference to the republican leader who has played such a decisive role. Brian Keenan has stated that there will be no decommissioning except the decommissioning of the British state in Ireland. He has insisted also that decommissioning will occur only after the establishment of a united socialist Ireland. This sets up the only relevant test for republican language. The new language does not constitute a definite break with the Keenan doctrine; it merely suggests that the movement may be giving these matters consideration.

For Mr Trimble and the Ulster Unionist Party the lessons are clear. This is precisely the moment to intensify his undoubted commitment to the agreement and the task of reaching a deal with nationalist Ireland. Mr Trimble has been here before. At the time of Heads of Agreement in January 1998, he persuaded Mr Blair that he was indispensable to the peace process and won the prime minister's support for his own broad conception of the deal. Over the next few weeks, an essentially passive, intellectually defensive unionist strategy was outflanked by the inevitable nationalist counter-attack, creating a crisis for Mr Trimble. He has now honourably met his commitments to his party; he has refuted the many cynics within his own community who doubted his integrity. But he now has some slight freedom of manoeuvre, and he must ask himself some basic questions, as must Mr Blair.

Last summer Mr Trimble did not believe Mr Blair's claim that there had been a seismic shift in republican thinking; in November, during the Mitchell review, he came to believe that Mr Adams and Mr McGuinness were sincere and could deliver on decommissioning. He took the risk of setting up the executive without decommissioning on that basis. He and Mr Blair will now have to re-evaluate. Because it may be that the republican movement, feeling itself spurned, may not now offer a timetable to decommission on any timescale which permits a resolution of the crisis.

Nor are the republicans willing to say that the war is over. All their actions are designed to allow – in the words of one senior US diplomat – an "escape hatch" which permits a return to armed struggle. It is not clear that the IRA accepts that the Ireland-wide vote on the agreement constituted a legitimate act of national self-determination. Ask any senior republican, Gerry Kelly say, and he will tell you he does not accept the doctrine of consent which asserts the democratic legitimacy of partition. This does not mean that the IRA actually wishes to return to sustained warfare. Ethnic rage has, for most of its middle-aged leaders, been replaced by ethnic vanity.

Any review will have to answer the question: what is the nature of Sinn Féin? Sinn Féin has turned out to be less ideologically supple than ministers and senior officials expected; but was there any reason for surprise? The agreement was brokered by the Ulster Unionist Party and the SDLP. Late on Good Friday itself, Sinn

Féin was not reconciled to the compromise, and it took two party conferences before it would accept the structures.

The PR brilliance of the Adams leadership has been in the subsequent assertion of ownership of the agreement against one of its principal authors, David Trimble, and one of its principal sponsors, the British government, culminating in the proposed legal action challenging Mr Mandelson's suspension. Mr Mandelson's action is in accord with the agreement's explicit assertion of the sovereignty of Westminster. The IRA has never been a party to the agreement and even after Friday's initiative is keeping its options open.

Nevertheless, there is hope for the agreement. It remains the fairest possible compromise between unionism and nationalism. But it cannot succeed on the basis of hype or illusion. The rest of Northern Irish society could have an interest in living with some republican ambiguities. But that would only be so if their fears, above all of living in a politically correct mafia state, were convincingly addressed by the British government.

ೞ ೞ ೞ

GETTING BACK TO THE BASICS OF CONSENT
Sunday Independent, 19 March 2000

The Clinton House is a honey-trap for Irish American nationalism. President Clinton has heaped flattery and prestige on Irish America in exchange for its growing opposition to the use of violence in the home country. Hailing the spirit of forgiveness and reconciliation exhibited by Nelson Mandela under great provocation, he has urged Irish Americans, a highly privileged and successful group after all, to follow the same path. Obviously, the White House was keen to see a breakthrough in the stalled peace process last week, but its hopes ran up against an obdurate reality.

From the moment of suspension of the executive, the Sinn Féin leadership has signalled that it was fearful of doing serious business on St Patrick's Day in Washington – that, in particular, it was not interested in any deal which involved a new deadline for decommissioning.

Strange times indeed, when David Trimble is more keen to perform proactively on the Washington stage – with a final explicit burial of his party's previous traditional position on prior decommissioning – than Gerry Adams. Mr Adams, revealingly, took refuge in talk of his "heavy schedule" when asked for a direct response to Mr Trimble's move.

Peter Mandelson will also have approached another US trip in a certain wry spirit. He knows that he is being accused of not signalling his intentions on suspension to Sinn Féin, leading them, apparently, to believe that they had no need to respond on the arms issue in the aftermath of Mr Trimble's decision to jump first and set up the executive. Yet in a private but entirely on-the-record meeting in New York before Christmas with some of the leading figures in Irish American journalism, Mr Mandelson signalled his intentions perfectly clearly. He might well be wondering why the message was not taken seriously.

But the lack of real progress in the US brings us back to the bitterly contested narrow ground at home. The agreement's broad structures represent the only realistic form of benign compromise between unionism and nationalism in Ireland. It is David Trimble's great achievement to have convinced a majority of the unionist population to this proposition.

He has been able to sustain the case for its structures even up to the point that the Paisleyite DUP was willing to operate them. But he was not able to sustain the case – nor did he wish to – for an agreement driven by the latent threat of force, in defiance of the agreement's most profound principles and his own, and for that matter the prime minister's, profound convictions on the matter.

Mr Trimble has another problem. The former first minister – as his recent expansive seminars at Boston College and Harvard confirmed – fully believes that the actual working of the executive, taken in the round, vindicates his view that the agreement is the basis of a stable Northern Ireland. But he is also aware that even many Trimbleist unionists do not agree: in particular, they perceive the *modus operandi* of the Sinn Féin ministers to be provocative, if inconsistent.

With what consistency after all can a Sinn Féin minister, happy to hold power under legislation which described all ministers as deriving their authority from Her Majesty, maintain an onslaught on the appearance of the union flag on government buildings in Northern Ireland? But the bad relations between the parties at least have a certain logic – sectarianism, for so long the life blood of the north's politics on all sides.

The two governments ought to be able to perform better. It is frankly amazing that 15 years after the signing of the Anglo-Irish Agreement, and three years after the election of an Hibernophile Labour government in Britain, that Anglo-Irish relations are so bad that an Irish government in deeply self-referential mode should think it intelligent to so publicly criticise Peter Mandelson's responsiveness to advice from senior figures in the security forces, while bombs continue to be assembled in the province. Even more revealing, even during the honeymoon period of the new executive, London-Dublin relations were poor.

Dublin, in British eyes, seemed to be slow to adjust to the new order, apparently believing it was possible and desirable to keep the first minister's office (and his SDLP deputy for that matter) out of the loop on some of the fundamental political issues of the day.

One former Irish premier, John Bruton, signalled last week his anxiety about the drift in Irish policy. To be fair, Dublin is caught on the horns of a dilemma. It genuinely wants stability in Ireland: this implies the preservation of Trimble.

But, on the other hand, the 1993-99 commitment to an inclusive settlement involving Sinn Féin, providing they decommission, has now, in effect, become what appears to many, no doubt unfairly, as a commitment to an inclusive settlement involving Sinn Féin, even if they never decommission.

But despite Dublin's protective concern, Sinn Féin is signalling that it is not in genuine negotiating mode and wants to play it long. Can there then be any hope for the Good Friday Agreement? In fact, the Ulster Unionist-Sinn Féin negotiation during the Mitchell review of 1999 was, it is now clear, a fairly spurious negotiation anyway.

This time it may be that the understanding which underpins any new setting up of the institutions (including Sinn Féin) will have to be between the British government, constitutional nationalism and the unionists – something along the lines of the Blair plan of last summer, offering certainty of sanction for the failure to decommission.

At the moment there is relatively little unionist enthusiasm for such a project, but at least they know that the British government has a principled position on the decommissioning issue. They also have a wider range of concerns (policing and ministerial autonomy are top of the list) which could be addressed entirely within the terms of the agreement.

Peter Mandelson believes that David Trimble and Seamus Mallon – the moderate centre – will determine the agenda for Northern Ireland of the agreement when it is up and running – he needs to convince those sections of moderate unionism who have their doubts based on the experience of the province's recent abortive experience of devolution.

Mr Trimble impulsively took a big risk in Washington: in so doing, he delighted the White House, the British government and even Mr Ahern. But he has offended and alarmed key sections of his own party at home on the eve of a crucial party conference, where he will be particularly vulnerable on the policing issue. Whatever the right and wrongs, the Patten report on the RUC has, as a matter of political reality, ended up by placing an unacceptably heavy burden on the agreement's chances of survival.

Policing reform, an issue which should be subordinate to the broader political process, has come to dominate it, precisely the outcome which should have been avoided at all costs. Mr Trimble is not going to be able to sustain this process, if Mr Mandelson remains in the grip of an over-optimistic assessment of the process thus far.

The basic concept of the agreement is clear – in return for unionist concessions on power-sharing and an Irish dimension, nationalism and republicanism accepted Northern Ireland's status as a legitimate part of the UK, based on consent. It needs to be renewed on all sides.

α α α

THE PRIZE OF PEACE IS WITHIN OUR GRASP
Sunday Independent, 7 May 2000

We have had spurious breakthroughs before. Last summer in Downing Street, the British government announced a breakthrough, which David Trimble was, in the end, unable to sustain. But unlike that Downing Street debacle, this time John Taylor has stayed at the heart of things. The prospects for eventual unionist support for this new deal must, on that account, be higher.

The language of the IRA statement is remarkably explicit. It is worth noting the relatively good tone on political matters. There is nothing wrong with a future in which "Irish republicans and unionists can, as equals, pursue our respective political objectives peacefully". This time the IRA does seem, at long last, to be signing up for the Good Friday Agreement.

The core of the IRA statement is clear: "We look to the two governments, and especially the British government, to fulfil their commitments under the Good Friday Agreement and the joint statement. To facilitate the speedy and full implementation of the Good Friday Agreement and the government's measures, our arms are silent and secure. There is no threat to the peace process from the IRA. In this context, the IRA leadership has agreed to put in place within weeks a confidence-building measure to confirm that our weapons remain secure. The contents of a number of our arms dumps will be inspected by agreed third parties, who will report that they have done so to the Independent International Commission on Decommissioning. The dumps will be re-inspected regularly to ensure that the weapons have remained silent."

Making all allowances for the fact that the agreed third parties have been as sensitively chosen from a republican point of view as is possible, this is still an important development.

The notion of dumping has an entirely respectable republican heritage, but – from a unionist point of view – this clearly seems to be putting arms beyond use. The world will say it is simply too good to pass up, but there will still be serious players within unionism who will attempt to reject this proposed new dispensation.

At the root of any chance of success is Mr Trimble's ability to convince the Ulster Unionist Council that he has won on the big philosophical issue. To many, Mr Trimble's priorities at times have seemed to be cranky, legalistic and pedantic, but he must soon be in a position to convince his constituency that his distinctive analysis goes right to the heart of the matter and that it has been vindicated.

For months, Mr Trimble has had a consistent message. He cannot accept the triumph of the Keenan doctrine. This is the notion associated with the prominent republican, Mr Brian Keenan, the doctrine that there will be no decommissioning except the decommissioning of the British state in Ireland. Mr Trimble's concept of the agreement is clear: in exchange for unionist concessions on power-sharing and the Irish dimension, nationalism accepts the legitimacy of Northern Ireland's place within the United Kingdom based on consent.

This means that on symbolic matters there is no requirement for an erasure of UK symbolism. But there must, of course, be a more sensitive use of these symbols as outlined, for example, in the Criminal Justice Review.

The Patten Report was so explosive for Mr Trimble, not so much because of its specific recommendations on policing matters, but because it seemed to reinforce the Keenan doctrine. Latterly the British government has begun to understand Mr Trimble's problem here – look at Mr Mandelson's recent speech at the Institute of Directors. In this speech, Mr Mandelson specifically denied that the agreement logically meant that Northern Ireland was to become a zone in which UK symbols were to be eliminated – the very notion explicitly defended by Chris Patten last September.

Some will see the leak of a British document, which included caustic comments on Mr Brian Cowen's insensitivity on this matter, as a cynical British move designed to raise Ulster unionist morale.

Maybe so – but it would be surprising if the document does not have a number of brothers and sisters. If Mr Trimble can convince the Ulster Unionist Council that his conception of the agreement has triumphed, he will win the day. Because it is that very conception which prompted the majority of the unionist community and political class to support the agreement in the first place.

Given the generally fraught state of Anglo-Irish relations in recent months, it is remarkable that a deal seems to have been achieved. If so, it reflects considerable credit on both governments. In the lead-up to the Good Friday Agreement, Mr Trimble held out to Mr Ahern the prospect of an end to the cold war on the island between north and south.

It was always a big prize for a democratic nationalist. It seems clear now that Mr Ahern is determined not to pass up on the opportunity. That prize is again within sight, but to realise it, Dublin and London will both have to keep their nerve over the next few inevitably rocky days.

Cઠ Cઠ Cઠ

THERE IS ONE THING OF WHICH WE CAN BE SURE TODAY – THIS IS NOT THE LAST CRISIS OF THE PEACE PROCESS

The Irish Times, 27 May 2000

In February 1951, Sir Basil Brooke, then the Prime Minister of Northern Ireland, addressed the Ulster Unionist Council. His message was an uncompromising one: unionism, faced with a Labour government at Westminster, had to modernise, move away from discriminatory practices or find a new leader.

In his diary, Brooke recorded: "I told them that the Convention on Human Rights compelled us to be fair to the minority, that I was not going to be responsible for discrimination.

"I finished off by saying that, if they wanted another administration who could perhaps solve these domestic problems from a new point of view, and if they thought we were not handling the socialist government right and wanted a government which would discriminate [against] Catholics, they could do so. I would not take on the job".

Brooke's approach helps to explain the otherwise inexplicable: his good relationship with senior socialists, like Herbert Morrison, a key cabinet figure and Peter Mandelson's grandfather.

Today, though David Trimble has resolutely refused the demagogy of "back me or sack me", he may well feel the same way. Does anyone in the Ulster Unionist Party have a better way of handling the Labour government?

Trimble is a proud man. It was difficult work behind the scenes to persuade him not to resign as first minister in the aftermath of Seamus Mallon's resignation as deputy first minister, even though that might well have finished the agreement there and then, as it was unlikely there were enough unionist assembly votes to place him back in office.

If he loses today, many will try to persuade him to stay on, pick up the pieces and salvage whatever can be salvaged.

They will have their arguments. Some unionist delegates who feel betrayed by Tony Blair still feel that Trimble is the best leader they have. Trimble is felt by some to lack the personal touch, but he is not as hated as Brian Faulkner was at the end of 1974. However, Trimble himself may well feel he has had enough – and with him, Ulster unionists would lose the first leader it has generated in the course of the troubles who has real credibility and respect within mainstream British public opinion.

Politically, David Trimble has had two great obsessions in the two years since the agreement was negotiated. One was the all-consuming game of high politics; negotiations involving Bill Clinton, Tony Blair and Bertie Ahern, Gerry Adams and Seamus Mallon, which took up so much of his time, leading to a neglect of such crucial matters as internal party reform. This is a neglect which may yet prove fatal if the block votes of the Orange Order and the rather more passionately anti-Trimble Young Unionists defeat him today.

The other great obsession was with the constitutional meaning of the agreement he had brokered: for Trimble it means, above all, that nationalist Ireland accepted the legitimacy of the union in exchange for a new deal on power-sharing and a north-south dimension.

Trimble's analysis of the constitutional meaning of the agreement is the clue to his current approach to the crisis. He is quite genuine in his belief that the Patten report's attitude towards British state symbolism is in conflict with the agreement.

He is equally genuine in his belief that Sinn Féin ministers hauling down the union flag in their departments are in conflict with the agreement. During a prolonged dialogue over several months, he had some considerable success in alerting Peter Mandelson to his difficulties and, indeed, some success in winning Mandelson over to his analysis.

Mandelson's clashes with Brian Cowen on this point – so memorably captured in the leaked British memorandum on the subject – became increasingly sharp from the beginning of March and gradually exploded into full public view at the end of April. As the Secretary of State put it this week, nationalists have to give more than lip service to the legitimacy of Northern Ireland's position in the United Kingdom.

But here is the rub. Many ordinary unionists have little interest in Trimble's constitutional niceties. They do not like the Patten report, not because it is incompatible with Trimble's interpretation of the agreement; they do not like it because they think it tends to legitimise terrorism against the forces of law and order.

They did not like the behaviour of Sinn Féin ministers – not because it was incompatible with Trimble's interpretation of the agreement, but because they found it sectarian, "in your face", undemocratic and a recipe for instability.

This is the clue to the recent failure of the unionist community to respond more warmly to the IRA statement, which genuinely broke new ground – a failure which surprised David Trimble himself and helps to explain his uncharacteristic hesitancy – now banished decisively in the last days of the campaign.

The weakness of the Trimble campaign, despite his numerous impressive media performances which made his opponents look mediocre and incoherent, was a reluctance to face up to this fact.

He controlled the argument on decommissioning: dumping, followed by inspection, is decommissioning by another name. He was helped by the government's many proposed changes to Patten, but he failed to counter unhappy memories of devolution in practice.

The *Trimbleistas* shrugged when pressed about the experience of the working executive – "a deal is a deal" – and they add that, if the unionist political class was not so divided, the party would have six ministers, instead of the four now promised if, as seems possible, the DUP withdraws from the executive.

They add that Bairbre de Brun's controversial decision to favour West Belfast maternity services over those of South Belfast was probably going to come from the direct rule administration anyway. One thing is clear, as one Stormont insider put it: "There is no point in giving Sinn Féin 60 per cent of the budget and then complaining when they begin to spend it".

More encouragingly, it is clear that the period of suspension has not been wasted – serious work has gone on which means that, for the first time in 30 years, the Ulster Unionist Party is equipped with developed policies on important matters of public policy.

Nevertheless, there has been a visceral Protestant reaction to Sinn Féin's possession of departments which touch so tangibly the lives of so many citizens. Jeffrey Donaldson was only ever effective when he slipped in the line about his two young children coming under the care of Martin McGuinness; the collective communal shudder was palpable.

This is the issue which, above all, hurt the Trimble campaign. Only late in the day was it addressed with conviction – in the leadership's letter to delegates and Trimble's interview in this newspaper with Frank Millar on the eve of the meeting. The case, in essence, was simply this: unless a more consensual style of executive work evolves, ministers will find themselves hamstrung forever on their key legislative projects.

As that reality began to sink in, the *Trimbleistas* believe that a more consensual style was genuinely evolving before the fall of the executive, but if they are wrong, the tides of protest – beginning with the South Antrim election and culminating in the general election – will destroy pro-agreement unionism and with it the agreement, even if Trimble carries the day today.

We can now be sure of only one thing about today's vote – it is not the last crisis of the peace process. Whether in or out of the executive, the DUP intends to keep up the pressure until, at least, the next general election. Council by-election results so far suggest that it has an alienated public opinion tending towards its view of things.

If Trimble finally runs out of luck – and worryingly, he has been incredibly lucky so far – what is lost? The Belfast Agreement? Trimble's own leadership? The whole project of new unionism?

Quite conceivably, all these disasters are just around the corner, but Trimble has one card. The 860 delegates who meet today have the decisive say. Every time they turn on the radio or the TV, they are told this, and it is true. If they vote Yes, Trimble can guarantee that their influence will be maintained, and they will be back to review progress or protest against the lack of it.

But if they vote No, this might be the last really important meeting of the Ulster Unionist Council; in short, it might well be the end of that organisation's profound and shaping influence on Northern Ireland's politics.

ೞ ೞ ೞ

UNIONISM FACES ITS STARKEST CHOICE
The Irish Times, 26 October 2000

As Ulster unionism threatens to implode and place both itself and the Belfast Agreement in the dustbin of history, one vital question is overdue for serious discussion. Where is the British government in all of this?

This crisis is nothing if not predictable. The probability of David Burnside's defeat in South Antrim was acknowledged by all serious commentators in early September. It provided the new element which gave credibility to Jeffrey Donaldson's challenge to the Ulster Unionists' policy direction – the fear of electoral meltdown for the party.

That fear may well be exaggerated; on the higher turnout of the general election, a seat like South Antrim should return to the Ulster Unionist fold.

Polls suggest that David Trimble has a respect across both sections of the community which no other Ulster Unionist can challenge. But the fear of meltdown is there, particularly for those local councillors who face the prospect of local elections next May.

By definition, a novel conjuncture requires a novel response, but response from London came there none. It is true that Peter Mandelson is apparently set to deliver to Mr Trimble's agenda on the flying of flags on government buildings and the RUC name on the title deeds of the new police force. But all this arises from a dialogue begun very intelligently by Mr Mandelson earlier in the year and is unrelated to the present crisis, except insofar as their delivery now, it is hoped, will calm nerves in the Trimble camp.

Making all allowances for the heavy objective constraints of the situation, this has certainly not been the most gloriously proactive phase in the history of the Northern Ireland Office. It has been remarkably passive as the crisis worsened.

Eloquent only in providing reasons why something cannot be done to help – even in those rare areas where there is an SDLP and Ulster Unionist commonality of interest – the NIO has made only one new intervention of note, and that an error of judgement. This was Peter Mandelson's perceived flirtation (in an interview with Ken Reid of UTV) with the threat of joint authority. I say perceived because Mr Mandelson is too shrewd a politician to use the actual words. Designed to help David Trimble, it backfired badly. Far from frightening unionists, it merely insulted them with a display of British bad faith.

It probably also strengthened the resolve of those republicans who think that Gerry Adams is in danger of surrendering too much ground. Why move on the arms issue if by not moving one will be rewarded by joint authority? Let us not forget that was Mr Adams' original objective when he launched his side of the peace process in the early 1990s.

For good measure, Mr Mandelson's intervention was less than enthusiastically received by Irish officials, who might reasonably have asked themselves, who was being insensitive to unionist feelings now? Yet, when this passivity received its inevitable reward – a move within the unionist party to close ranks around a compromise motion which would likely impose impossible deadlines on the process – the London reaction was one of surprise and, understandably, concern.

Nobody believes that the republican movement with its current difficulties in west Belfast will react sympathetically to any Ulster Unionist move away from the May deal which set up the executive – a deal endorsed narrowly by the Ulster Unionist Council earlier this year.

More importantly, a unilateral breaking of the terms of the understanding of May gives the republican movement the high ground – a high ground which it visibly lacked at the time of the February suspension when it was the republican movement which was widely perceived to have reneged unilaterally on an understanding.

Mr Trimble has, as he repeated endlessly in recent days, a bottom line on decommissioning. But he wishes to be left in control of the timing of that agenda, because timing is the clue to winning the inevitable conflict with the republican movement, which will not want to go beyond the arms inspections already granted.

The IRA's confirmation yesterday that it will allow a further arms dump inspection at a date to be specified may be dismissed by the Donaldson faction as an empty, cynical public relations gesture. Maybe so, but the reality is that no IRA member will ever use those dumps again.

The new inspection will allow the process to be seen as a real one. It is one of the many worries of the present crisis that the inspections process has been so rubbished in recent weeks that the inspections currently work for Jeffrey Donaldson's cause and not David Trimble's. This is an absurdity, and any new inspection would provide the perfect moment to exhibit the serious nature of the process.

We are in for a dramatic 72 hours. Today's visit by Tony Blair will at least serve to remind Ulster Unionist Council delegates that the perceived realities in Antrim, Carrickfergus and Larne are not the only realities which count; a unionist by definition has to be concerned with the realities in London.

But there is a point to be made on the other side. The fatwa against the anti-agreement unionists has been the greatest error of government policy against the referendum. A constituency – many of whom were seized by genuine moral doubt – was treated as if it comprised unrepentant bigots who could be marginalised.

It is time for some mending of fences. Machiavelli argues in *The Prince* that a powerful leader can easily afford to break his pledges. But Machiavelli also argued that this could only be done when the circumstances which caused these promises to be given no longer applied.

In the case of Northern Ireland, the circumstances which caused Mr Blair at the time of the reform to articulate so brilliantly a vision of a political future free from the threat of violence still apply – even more sharply now than they did in 1998.

The timing of this debate does not suit Mr Trimble. An extra week would have allowed a fuller public debate. But the delegates should remember one thing: they have a stark alternative. Either implode or play it long and place the real problem of the process back at the door of the two governments and the republican movement, as they did between November 1999 and February 2000.

Joint authority is not just around the corner, but a bleak political future is. This is a future in which unionists cease to make history and allow it to be made by other forces and traditions – forces and traditions which have no reason to hold unionist concerns at heart.

Cℨ Cℨ Cℨ

BLAIR AND CLINTON COULD SINK ULSTER'S CHANCE FOR PEACE

The Daily Telegraph, 22 May 2001

Bill Clinton has returned to Ireland. He is expected to discuss the current serious difficulties afflicting the Belfast agreement with Tony Blair later this week. Both men are genuinely keen to preserve that agreement, but they need to be careful that their activities over the next few days and weeks do not have the effect of undermining it.

Both former president and prime minister are 1960s children, in the sense that they analyse the Ulster troubles in terms of the Deep South in the pre-civil rights era. Mr Clinton's language, in particular, resonates with this assumption and, over time, the choreography of his visits, initially well-balanced, has veered off into a markedly Irish nationalist direction.

If either Mr Clinton or Mr Blair had actually marched on civil rights marches, they would know that this analogy was misleading. In particular, the presence of an unresolved national question makes the process of internal reform spectacularly difficult for any state, denying it the very legitimacy that it needs to effect change.

The reform of America has been made easier by the fact that there was never any question of the absorption of the United States into another political entity. Unionist opponents of the agreement are enjoying the opportunity to attack a "pledge-breaking" prime minister and a discredited former president. On 3 March 1999, the prime minister told the *Scotsman* that IRA decommissioning must happen because "people have got to know if they are sitting down in the executive with people who have given up violence for good".

Sinn Féin is now in its second year in the executive, and a senior republican, Brian Keenan – with the full approval of the Sinn Féin leadership – has recently pointedly reminded us that violence has not been given up for good. Interestingly, British public opinion appears to be increasingly dissatisfied – with 75 per cent saying that the IRA must decommission if Sinn Féin is to stay in the executive.

President Clinton, on the other hand, at the end of June 1999 assured unionists that they could "simply walk out" if the IRA commitments on decommissioning were not kept. When, in effect, David Trimble did just that, at the beginning of 2000, the president exerted – unsuccessfully – his influence against Mr Trimble.

Unlike anti-agreement politicians, Mr Trimble has inevitably more complex attitudes towards the two leaders. Both Mr Blair and Mr Clinton have defended in explicit terms the constitutional outlines of the historic compromise settlement that Mr Trimble is proud to have negotiated. They have defended it in terms that accept that unionist core interests have to be, and have been, protected.

But the first minister is well aware that Mr Clinton and Mr Blair have left him in a rather exposed position at the present time. The Ulster Unionist Party manifesto, launched yesterday, makes the point: "We regret that others play down the threat to peace and democracy from paramilitaries and have so far failed to deliver their pledges."

It is, of course, something that the electorate has noticed. The key group in this election comprises those erstwhile pro-agreement unionist supporters who now feel let down. There are senior officials who believe that the Ulster middle class is privately grateful to the "man in Whitehall" for taking on the inevitable morally ambiguous burdens of peace negotiations.

But the Ulster middle class does not feel grateful. The Faith and Politics group – a distinguished body of pro-agreement Catholic and Protestant clergy – has concluded recently that many people feel that their "moral universe" has been "turned upside down". It is not a nice feeling.

This is why Mr Trimble explicitly stated, when last sharing a platform with President Clinton: "There cannot be a moral vacuum at the heart of the peace process. That is why I stand firm on the need for decommissioning." This is why Mr Trimble announced his decision to resign on 1 July if the second official target date for decommissioning is passed without action. Mr Trimble's action was dictated, above all, by a desire to show to the people of Ulster that, even if the other actors in the drama were not morally serious, he was.

It was an action that stunned the Northern Ireland secretary, John Reid. His officials presumably recalled the young diplomat Niccolo Machiavelli's explanation in similar circumstances 500 years ago: "I am dealing with a prince who manages things for himself, and it is therefore extremely difficult to know what he means to do."

In the same report, Machiavelli pointed out how weakness could be a kind of strength. Mr Trimble has been forced by the other players to carry the principal political burdens of the peace process. In consequence, everyone else has become more dependent on him. He has had to face an election without IRA decommissioning, because it suited the republicans to create division within unionist ranks rather than their own. The prime minister, reluctantly, has been complicit in this development. Moreover, in the aftermath of the election, Mr Trimble had no firm reason to expect any positive developments.

But a point has now been reached where, insofar as any one man is carrying the strain and stresses of a complex political structure, it is Mr Trimble. Some in the government simply assume that the strain will break him and that the whole process will shortly go "belly up". But it is a little early to say that.

Mr Trimble has made himself more popular than the agreement and, while his party has serious problems in certain localities, the broad picture in the polls is reassuring. Polls in Ulster traditionally underplay hardline sectarian sentiment, but, if they are not lying too much, Mr Trimble will still be a force after the election. This will give the British and Irish governments a chance to save the agreement – but they can do it only by facing up to the decommissioning question at last.

But do the governments have the qualities necessary to pull it off? At any rate, they have the negative vision of the meltdown in the Middle East to encourage them in their task.

ᘉ ᘉ ᘉ

TRIMBLE'S SURPRISE TACTIC PAYS OFF
The Sunday Times, 3 June 2001

"Has Trimble any further surprises up his sleeve?" Bill Clinton asked during his last days as American president.

We now know the resourceful Ulster unionist leader had at least one: his decision to resign as first minister if the Good Friday Agreement's deadline for decommissioning at the end of June passed without IRA action. It would mean new assembly elections, but is the only way of preserving the devolved institutions for the summer.

Although the battle within nationalism is important, David Trimble is the commanding figure of this electoral campaign. His resignation decision, made in principle some months ago, was not because of his assessment of the mood of the electorate. Rightly or wrongly, he believed his private polling, which is now supported by other public polls. He has long been convinced there will be no UUP meltdown in the general election. The decision was based on his assessment of the mood of the Provisional IRA and the British and Irish governments.

Let us recall the history of this problem. With his first post-dated resignation letter Trimble, in effect, forced the suspension of the institutions in February 2000. It was a remarkable achievement – the UUP leader compelled an uncertain British government to defy the White House and the Irish government. In the end, most MPs supported a suspension as the only possible response to the IRA's failure to "jump together" on devolution and decommissioning as it promised.

It is arguably one of Trimble's big political errors that he did not make enough of this victory when talking to his own people. If he had driven home the lesson harder, his position might be stronger today. But he was determined to protect the agreement and minimise nationalist and republican alienation.

During the suspension in February 2000, however, republican sympathisers advanced a new line of argument that clearly had an impact with the British government. Republicans, it was said, had insufficient time to prepare their people for decommissioning. It might have been different, it was said, if Sinn Féin had been in its second year of government when the tough decision came.

Second time around, Trimble has been determined, despite brutal opposition from his own party, to allow the republican movement the necessary time. Sinn Féin ministers are now well into their second year of office. They clearly love it. In Trimble's assessment, republicans will only act to save their positions at Stormont if it is clear that they stand to lose a broad public relations battle by not acting. They lost the argument over suspension in 2000, and that is why they offered the concession of arms inspection and the promise – as yet unfulfilled – to move on putting weapons beyond use.

Many in the media insist the IRA does not respond to unionist challenges. Significantly, however, republicans have not reacted to Trimble's move by going off in a huff. Instead, last week, they continued to accept that decommissioning is an obligation under the agreement. They are dropping hints, yet again, that the matter can be resolved if further concessions on policing and demilitarisation are made. The effect of Trimble's action has thus far been salutary.

The British government also appears to have rediscovered the significance of the June target date, set last May. It is right to do so. But a large responsibility lies with the Irish government.

A struggle is going on for the soul of Irish nationalism, not just on the electoral battlefields of West Tyrone but more profoundly in Government Buildings in Dublin. The SDLP and the Irish government have traditionally embraced a conciliatory tradition where the emphasis is on co-operation with unionists in order to lower barriers and bring about Irish unity by consent.

The republican tradition is very different. Throughout the Troubles it attempted unsuccessfully to coerce unionists into a united Ireland. Today, republicans take refuse in a wager on the Catholic birth rate, which tacitly concedes that they cannot think of any good reason why a Protestant might be a nationalist. In Sinn Féin's recent utterances, Wolfe Tone's unity of Catholic, Protestant and dissenter is a lost dream.

For Dublin, this is a critical moment: either be drawn into a narrow tribal agenda – which will threaten stability – or draw on the most profound of the aspirations which have contributed to the making of the Irish state.

Republicans must be redirected back to the world of political compromise and decommissioning. In the afterglow of an election in which Sinn Féin expects to advance, will there ever be a better moment?

One underlying reality is in danger of being forgotten in the midst of all the electoral rhetoric. All the parties are happy in the new Stormont. Last week, Ian Paisley spoke of wading into the Boyne; this week, Peter Robinson speaks merely of recasting the agreement.

Such a change of tone presumably reflects the mood on the doorsteps. Robinson's strategy is clear: a formal renegotiation and then substantive acceptance. But would the DUP fundamentalists allow this? Would nationalists dream of humouring the DUP and letting them off the hook? Very few – outside Robert McCartney's camp – want to destroy devolution, but the DUP devolutionists could end up destroying it despite themselves.

Westminster will be a rubber stamp for a huge Labour majority in the next five years. From a democratic point of view, a local parliament will be all the more attractive. But the law of unintended consequences – starting with those voters who stay at home on Thursday – is one of the most powerful laws in politics.

ෆ ෆ ෆ

TRIMBLE STEPS DOWN – AND INTO A NEW KIND OF POWER
The Daily Telegraph, 2 July 2001

When David Trimble first visited the Somme battlefield some years ago, he was visibly moved. Perhaps he was thinking of his grandfather, "Captain Jack", who was lucky enough to survive the war, perhaps of the many who died. But it is also clear that he was contemplating the political lessons. The Somme was a massive Ulster Protestant sacrifice on behalf of the United Kingdom – 5,500 died on the first two days; by the end hardly a family in the province was untouched. It was the moment of the maximum integration of Ulster loyalism with the United Kingdom as a whole.

But 1916 saw another sacrifice based on an entirely different ideology. Irish republican separatism, with a death toll in the low hundreds: the Easter Rising in Dublin. Yet, within five years it was to be clear that it was the Easter Rising, not the Somme, which drove London's political agenda. In November 1920, Ulster unionists came under pressure from London to accept some form of Irish unity outside the United Kingdom. The unionist leader, Sir James Craig, extracted himself from this pressure only by the deftest footwork and a willingness to reach radical compromises with Sinn Féin, such as the two Craig-Collins pacts of 1922.

His keen historical understanding of this period is the clue to Mr Trimble's activism. His predecessor, Lord Molyneaux, eschewed high wire acts; Mr Trimble himself has never been off the high wire. He has no regrets today about his course of action. He has always believed that London's incessant search for an understanding with Irish nationalism left him with no option. He has demonstrated before the world that a substantial section of the unionist population was ready to support a generous historic compromise with their nationalist neighbours. The political structures he negotiated were not the cause of his recent electoral difficulties. There is indeed a widespread tacit acceptance of these structures, stretching to Ian Paisley's Democratic Unionist Party. Mr Trimble's electoral setbacks were due to other causes. One is the implementation of the Patten police reform, which, while yet to win nationalist support for the police, comprehensively alienated the unionist community. Then there is the growing willingness of the British government to accept the IRA's narrow definition of a ceasefire – no attacks on soldiers or police – a move away from Tony Blair's referendum commitment that all killings and beatings should cease. The IRA's blunt refusal to decommission has brought this problem into even sharper relief.

But are we on the terrain of a new and striking double paradox? Is Mr Trimble's weakness his strength? Is the strength of Gerry Adams becoming his weakness? It is typical of Mr Trimble's quirky originality as a politician that, at the moment of his resignation as first minister, he is setting the agenda. In the past few days, he has seen the British, Irish and American governments row in behind his demand for decommissioning with a renewed vigour. John Hume and the SDLP tell the IRA to do it and do it now. Interestingly, he has frustrated his opponents within unionism. Mr Trimble's decision to resign places him firmly on the middle ground of modern unionism and leaves those who wish to depose him looking as though they can only respond to his initiatives. The DUP's modernisers can only fret as Dr Paisley, who has taken his party's recent electoral success as a personal vindication, turns up the rhetorical volume. Any strategy to blame Mr Trimble for all the heavy costs unionists have paid in helping establish the institutions of the agreement while, at the same time, moving in on them, has taken a severe knock. Irony of ironies, Mr Trimble yesterday left the executive set up by the Belfast Agreement, but his DUP opponents remain within it, prisoners of his policy.

Mr Adams is certainly in a strong position. He has surprised even himself by the success of his electoral strategy north and south. Nobody seriously believes that he has to bow now either to the IRA army council or the base of the republican movement. What happens next on decommissioning will be determined by Mr Adams himself and a few other senior republican strategists. How will they calculate their interests are best served?

They might well believe that their electoral triumphs north and south will continue anyway, regardless of whether or not there is decommissioning. Brian Keenan, a senior republican, has already expressed support for such an interpretation.

They might well believe that further radical British concessions are on the agenda. In this context they will have been encouraged by some loose language on the British side. But here lie dangers for republicans. Joint authority is not in the material interests of London, and it is for that reason that London possesses no serious long-term strategy to implement it. British withdrawal is vastly easier to dream about than to achieve. The Irish political establishment has been upset by Sinn Féin's role in the recent Nice referendum defeat. The same policy elite which did so much to advance Sinn Féin has now been stung by the very viper it clutched so warmly to its bosom. An angry and thwarted Irish state remains a potent obstacle to Sinn Féin aspirations. Without decommissioning, Irish democracy will become all too keenly aware that it has a truculent new force at the centre of its politics, a new force that does not accept the democratic rules of the game. In this sense Mr Trimble's problem has become their problem.

The long-term logic of Mr Adams' political career in recent years is clear enough: this logic implies that the Sinn Féin leader will move, as he did during the last suspension, to protect the agreement's institutions, to which he has described himself a "convert". In this scenario, the IRA makes a limited offer on de-commissioning in exchange for further concessions on policing and demilitarisation. Mr Blair, then, will be asked to swallow his referendum pledge of "no local policing" in favour of the highly controversial Patten recommendation of private local agencies. The republican leadership would then sell its own move to its foot soldiers as a minimal concession while insisting that everyone else treat Sinn Féin as a party of the purest democratic integrity.

This is the logic of its position, but the republican movement is today dizzy with success and anxious to topple the one serious unionist leader thrown up by the Troubles. The underlying logic will operate only if the governments make clear that failure to move on decommissioning will carry a serious political penalty. Mr Blair has a role to play here, but the heaviest burden is on Bertie Ahern. Following Seamus Mallon's brave words yesterday, the Irish prime minister has a stark choice. He can defend the core liberal principles of Irish political life, or he can surrender to the darker forces of blood-and-soil nationalism. Mr Ahern has to place himself in the front line of the struggle for decommissioning. If he does not, the Belfast Agreement is heading for the dustbin of history. Not for nothing did one of the most influential mandarins of Anglo-Irishry grimly recall last week General de Gaulle's dictum that treaties are like pretty young girls, they last as long as they last.

C3 C3 C3

HISTORY IS NEVER OVER IN NORTHERN IRELAND
The Times, 30 October 2001

The press responded enthusiastically to the breakthrough in the Irish conflict. "Blessed are the peacemakers," cried the *Daily Express*. *The Times* welcomed the "refreshing spectacle" of a "settlement" of a "longstanding dispute", especially at "a period in the world's history in which reason and legality have repeatedly been overborne by emotional violence".

Ministers from Belfast and Dublin quickly got together to discuss matters of common concern. The prime minister immediately attempted to apply the same approach to bringing about stability in the Middle East.

When did all this happen? Last week? No, though the reader might be forgiven for thinking so. It was the last week of April 1938. Neville Chamberlain had just signed the Anglo-Irish agreement of that year with Eamon de Valera. British imperialism and Irish republicanism were, at last, it was said, reconciled.

Such hopes were to be sadly disappointed. If there is reason for Blairite caution and avoidance of hubris after last week's triumph, it lies here. The knock-on international effect of Anglo-Irish reconciliation appears to be rather limited. But let us be clear – a policy on Ireland which senior officials were honest enough to describe as a form of appeasement – appears to be on the verge of success. A new Northern Ireland, more stable than anything experienced in the past generation, may be just around the corner.

The decommissioning issue entered public debate to some degree accidentally in late 1993. It reflected the desire of the Major government to avoid an open break in its relationship with James Molyneaux's Ulster Unionists after the unexpected revelation of the government's secret talks with the IRA. But it also reflected more profoundly a requirement of any credible democracy. The notion of a party of government which retained its private army fully intact and dishing out violence to its enemies was too ghastly to be contemplated.

At the beginning of 1994, Gerry Adams publicly warned Sinn Féin that both the British and Irish governments expected IRA decommissioning as part of any peace deal. Martin McGuinness was known to have confessed in October 1994 to the Irish prime minister: "We know the arms will have to be banjaxed". If the IRA – contrary to its later claims – was well aware of this reality, even before its first ceasefire, why has it taken seven long years to achieve it? The answer lies in the hyper-cautious style of two men – Gerry Adams and Tony Blair.

Long after he knew he had the necessary majority within his own movement, Mr Adams delayed decommissioning. Long after it seemed the mainstream IRA was unlikely to bomb London again, Tony Blair remained concerned. Most Sinn Féin leaders wanted to protect the political gains made through the working of the Good Friday Agreement – but the destruction of David Trimble's leadership of unionism was also an exciting alternative project. In such a context, republican hardliners could always argue the case for one more negotiation.

Hence Mr Trimble's decision to resign as first minister earlier this year: a decision which, alone, has allowed him to retain control of his party. A collapse of the agreement, which left him in place as the leader of Ulster unionism, was a considerably less enticing prospect for republicans. Even so, the process would have been strung out for another few months. But events in Colombia – where the IRA got itself entangled with narco-terrorists – and the September 11 atrocities combined to close down Sinn Féin's options.

What now for Northern Ireland? If Mr Trimble scrapes through this week and is re-elected first minister, it will unleash a fierce debate within Ian Paisley's Democratic Unionist Party. Mr Paisley and his party have been prematurely written off before. The truth is that as long as he draws breath, he and his party will be a substantial force in Northern Irish politics. Nevertheless, the struggle for hegemony within unionist politics appears to be nearing its end with Mr Trimble as close to victory as he has ever been.

Sinn Féin's "peace" strategy has been based on the notion of bringing about a debilitating split within unionism. It is to be found in a published prison letter from Danny Morrison to Gerry Adams, and it is also to be found, crucially, in the celebrated TUAS (Tactical Use of Armed Struggle) document, circulated to IRA volunteers in the mid-1990s. For much of the past three years since the agreement was signed Sinn Féin has, indeed, been able to drive the process in such a way as to accentuate divisions within the unionist community. It is unlikely that Sinn Féin will abandon that strategy, but it may find that in the new circumstances created by decommissioning, that it is not so effective.

This is not even now the "end of history", Northern Irish-style, but there are significant omens. The Good Friday Agreement has regained some of the legitimacy it lost among moderate unionists since the referendum in May 1998. Unionist-SDLP relations are better than for years. The chasm between the mainstream IRA and republican dissidents remains significant.

Mr Trimble's speech to the Conservative Party this autumn and his call to the Labour Party to allow membership in Northern Ireland signals a strong desire to move beyond the age-old quarrel in Northern Ireland. It may be aspirational at this stage, and it can easily be thwarted by events. But it shows the glimmer of a hope for a different style of politics in Northern Ireland, in which the discourse is not permanently dominated by parochial, sectarian considerations.

Of course, Northern Ireland will continue to face both ways in terms of its long-term aspirations; the trick will be to accept that fact and make it less destructive in its implications.

ଔ ଔ ଔ

Unionist Fears Are Not Based on Sectarianism

The Irish Times, 15 January 2002

The British state is puzzled. Why, it asks, can unionists not make more of their victories: the principle of consent, the return of Stormont, and decommissioning? The police reforms may have been hard to swallow, but everyone knows that former RUC officers will be the backbone of the new force for many years to come. The irony is that if the reforms work, they will merely bring about the situation desired in the early years of the unionist government – a police force with a substantial Catholic presence.

Why, the British ask, does unionism insist on dwelling neurotically on its apparent setbacks? Does it not see that the concession of Westminster facilities to Sinn Féin is a concession only "on the margin"? Indeed, as Kate Hoey MP shrewdly pointed out in the debate, it represents the conversion of Sinn Féin to, if not exactly to a unionist, then at least to a Redmondite view of the centrality of Westminster in Irish affairs.

The IRA campaign was, after all, based on the attempt to destroy the consent principle. Its greatest political victory was to blow away Stormont, and the IRA leadership has always insisted, until now, that even a token act of decommissioning would represent a surrender.

The *Trimbleista* response to this argument is invariably one of irritation. One senior Stormont figure muttered: "Don't they have any understanding what it is like to have Martin McGuinness as a Minister of Education?" The recently published biography of Mr McGuinness has revived painful memories.

Mr Trimble's supporters ask if London is so self-absorbed that it has no capacity for empathy. More seriously, has it taken on board the political arithmetic of the great victory in the referendum in 1998? Then, only a small majority of unionists could bring themselves to support the agreement. A significant proportion of

the unionist "Yes" voters believed there would be no legitimisa-
tion of the terrorist campaign that appeared to be coming, falter-
ingly, to an end. They anticipated that the subsequent months
would see a steady but perceptible erosion of terrorist organisa-
tions and of the terrorist mentality.

But, counters the voice of the British and Irish governments,
this can all be done in time. Just look at de Valera's progress from
the "slightly constitutional" to the constitutional politician and
reformed revolutionary.

But de Valera's own reflections in 1957 on this matter give us
some clue as to the weakness of this argument and help to explain
why matters remain so fraught. The perceived enemy in the 1919-
21 War of Independence campaign was the British presence. De
Valera, commenting on the IRA campaign launched in 1956,
viewed it as an inter-Irish civil war. In our latest campaign of
communal conflict, the troubles, republicans inflicted the bulk of
the killings (2,139 deaths), while suffering themselves 392 of the
fatal casualties.

The legacy of bitterness is substantial. In the eight decades following the Irish civil war, when did Fine Gael and Fianna Fáil
overcome their residual bitterness and enter government together?

It is as well to say these things openly. The agreement has to
be the only civilised way to move the north forward. But it will
not be served by a failure to grasp the nature of the persistent cri-
ses which constantly grip it, nor to underestimate the crisis of legitimacy it has in the eyes of a large section of the unionist community. This is not a simple expression of unionist sectarianism,
as so many believe. Sectarianism among unionists there certainly
is, as the recent explosion of hatred in north Belfast reveals for all
to see. The simple truth is, however, that David Trimble could not
have got half so far as he has if an exclusivist sectarianism had
been the driving dynamic of the unionist community.

Not one of those writers whose stock in trade has been the denunciation of unionist sectarianism came close to predicting the course of the last five years – the negotiation of the agreement and the successful establishment of a power-sharing government. These writers also fail to see how much of the distrust of the agreement derives from the best and not just the worst instincts of the unionist community.

In the interests of peace and power-sharing, we have a form of government that ensures representation for former terrorists. So be it. But some preoccupations of the "No" voter – having a political party with guns exercising power, the issue of crimes that go unpunished, paramilitarism on the margins, and the interpenetration of political power and crime – are crucial to many ordinary unionist "Yes" voters, too. The surest way to tip the balance of opinion against the agreement is to ignore them.

It is necessary, however, to be honest. Not all the problems of the agreement can be laid at the door of either the British government or the republicans. In a recent interview in *Parliamentary Brief*, David Trimble acknowledged how unprepared unionists were for a return to government. "We talked a good game," he says drily.

Mistakes were made, and the unionist performance in government has not been strong enough to shift sentiment in their own community. The solid core of support for the agreement which remains, remains principally because it regards the agreement as the necessary form of historic compromise which is the most reliable way of preserving the union.

This is hardly surprising. Most of the political energy of the unionist community has been devoted to an internal, debilitating feud. In such a context, some of the hoped-for positive effects of the agreement do not appear to have materialised. There is no sign, for example, that young Protestants are less likely to leave Northern Ireland and take up university places in the rest of the UK. The return of the "respectable upper middle classes" to unionist politics, while significant in some constituencies, has been a patchy process thus far.

And there are fears – exaggerated, say some academic demographers – about the relative demographic decline of the Protestant community. If the latest survey evidence is even remotely correct, it could well be in the unionist interest to see the results of a border poll. But instinctively – ever since Brian Faulkner turned down Edward Heath's offer of one in 1971 – unionists have disliked border polls, regarding them as destabilising. Faulkner went down a different route, which included the illusion of the retention of security powers. This led to a humiliating defeat, but the lesson has never been fully grasped.

We are entering a critical phase. In his recent Liverpool University speech, Dr Reid bravely attempted to address the issue of unionist alienation. His speech may well be seen in the long run to have had a profound significance as the first sign of the British government's awareness of the scale of the problem. But framed as it was for a formal academic environment, it lacked bite. Above all, it lacked an explicit acknowledgement that there may be such a thing as a siege mentality, but there is also such a thing as a besieging behaviour.

Why is this moment of such importance? The high water mark of concessions to republicans will soon be reached when the government delivers amnesties to paramilitaries on the run and further extensions of the inquiry culture. At this point, the issue becomes: does the British state have the resolve to protect the settlement in Northern Ireland?

In principle, it has the room to manoeuvre, as since September 11 fears about an IRA return to violence have diminished markedly. In spite of the way the agreement was sold in Northern Ireland as marking the end of violence, fears of a return to violence seem to have exercised a surprisingly strong influence over the considerations of the British government since 1998. But the events in the US must surely mark a watershed.

One of the great advantages of the agreement is that it has moved the political and ideological struggle to the forefront. In this respect, it has fulfilled its promise. But the devolution experiment throughout the UK is not working in quite the way advertised by Dr Reid in Liverpool. Indeed, it is clear from the new British Social Attitude Survey that the new devolved constitutional settlement has actually eroded a sense of Britishness throughout the UK. In his recent Castlereagh lecture on the 1801 Act of Union in the House of Lords, Mr Trimble noted how the patchy history of the union can be attributed, in part, to the lack of interest in London to devoting the intellectual and political resources to making the project work. A similar fear now haunts the workings of the new constitutional settlement: it is one thing – in 1800 as in 2001 – for London to establish new structures for the union; it is another thing to breathe life into them.

It is increasingly obvious that Mr Trimble's analysis of the evolution of the republican movement was correct. But his recent remarks display a renewed concern about the British state. Quite simply, does it have a bottom line, or will it continue to allow, by default, the republican movement to impose an ideologically green tinge on what is, institutionally, a structural, unionist deal?

છ છ છ

FIGHTING FOR GOOD FRIDAY
Financial Times, 17 September 2002

David Trimble, Northern Ireland's first minister, is once again in trouble with his supporters. On Saturday, the Ulster unionist leader must justify his strategy, and by implication his leadership, at another meeting of his party's ruling council, the ninth such occasion since he negotiated the Good Friday Agreement in April 1998.

Mr Trimble has prevailed at each of these meetings, if only by the tiniest of margins. But this time there is a real chance he will not. Cracks have appeared in the once loyal Ulster Unionist group in the Northern Ireland assembly. Most worrying, opinion in the broader unionist electorate has turned against the agreement, even if it is not clear whether ordinary unionists want their party to withdraw from government.

Mr Trimble's critics within his party, notably the Westminster MPs Jeffrey Donaldson and David Burnside, have a compelling argument with which Mr Trimble sympathises. They want to know how unionists can legitimately tolerate obvious IRA violations of the agreement, such as its activities in Colombia or the theft of intelligence information from Castlereagh police station.

But Mr Trimble's critics have one big weakness: they do not have a clue what to do next. They dream about a form of devolution that denies Sinn Féin a place in the administration of the province. That was always implausible. It became inconceivable as soon as Sinn Féin overtook the moderate nationalist SDLP at last year's general election to become the majority party for nationalists. The only real alternative to the agreement is a return to direct rule – a form of administration involving a significant role for Dublin following the 1985 Anglo-Irish agreement.

The more moderate critics within the Ulster Unionists might contemplate a collapse of the agreement and a return to direct rule – but only with Mr Trimble leading the party and only once the blame had been firmly pinned on the republican movement. A Donaldson-Burnside victory now would isolate unionism from mainstream British opinion and reduce its influence over any new experiment in joint London-Dublin rule over the province.

It is often said that Mr Trimble has failed to sell the agreement in a positive way to the unionist community. It was always unrealistic to expect him to promote it with undiluted enthusiasm. A recent opinion poll, the Northern Ireland Life and Times survey, tells us why: most Protestants do not see devolution as integral to their prosperity; they do not think devolved government provides value for money; and while they accept that the agreement's collapse would lead to more sectarian violence, they do not believe the agreement's survival will lead to less. The survey also shows levels of communal antagonism to have increased.

These facts, worrying though they are, do not entirely damn the agreement. Mr Trimble can point to the collapse of the republican movement's core project, the coercion of Ulster's Protestants into a united Ireland. The contrast between the horror of the IRA's terrorist campaign and the banality of Sinn Féin's largely conventional role in the assembly has yet to penetrate fully into the unionist body politic.

There is still a problem of republican paramilitarism. Gerry Adams, the Sinn Féin president, may have chosen the path of political compromise, but he controls the republican movement by permitting its militaristic adventures so as to sustain the illusion that a return to armed struggle is still possible.

Mr Adams thereby imposes the costs of his own man-management on Mr Trimble. The republican leadership does not want to go back to war, but it heads a movement that instinctively prefers tension to normality in the province.

Mr Trimble should be able to turn this situation to his advantage. There is no alternative to some form of engagement with Sinn Féin. So old-style Ulster unionism, cantankerous but strategically inept, will no longer do.

The creation of a ceasefire monitoring body should give his supporters some heart. It is a step forward for Mr Trimble's strategy of shifting the focus to the IRA: it either controls its zealots or it takes responsibility for collapsing the institutions of devolved government.

Even if he wins on Saturday, the first minister is not out of the woods. The next assembly elections, set for May 2003, may polarise opinion in the province to the extent of destroying the Good Friday Agreement. Mr Trimble wants the British government to hold a referendum on the future status of Northern Ireland within the UK in order to improve turnout and rally moderates behind devolution. Essentially, voters would be asked to tolerate de-volved government with Sinn Féin ministers as the most practical way of sustaining the union.

There is little sign yet that the British and Irish governments accept Mr Trimble's argument. But nor do they have any answer to the questions likely to be thrown up by next May's election.

જ જ જ

SINN FÉIN MUST NOW CONFRONT THE SCALE OF ITS OWN POLITICAL AMBITIONS
Sunday Independent, 20 October 2002

You have to hand it to Tony Blair. The peace process to which he had devoted so much energy enters crisis. What does the British prime minister do? Sit on his hands and say "woe is me?" Not a bit of it. He rushed to Belfast to deliver a speech which is designed to turn the whole course of history and get the Belfast agreement back on a stable footing.

Some of the sound bites were a little tired – "The crunch is the crunch", for example. Some of the tone was awkward and even mawkish, irritating in equal measure to nationalists and unionists. But there was no mistaking the prime minister's fundamental message.

He broke decisively with the approach to the peace process embodied in his last major Belfast speech at Stranmillis. There the issue was defined as unionists having to demonstrate a commit-ment to power-sharing, while republicans had to demonstrate a commitment to peace. On Thursday, Mr Blair explicitly stated that David Trimble's wing of unionism had demonstrated good faith and a commitment to power-sharing, but republicans had yet to demonstrate a commitment to completely peaceful methods. The Blair wager on Trimble was visibly still in place.

For a Dublin establishment increasingly disinclined to do business with Mr Trimble, it was a thought-provoking message. But Downing Street was well aware of the figures in the BBC poll last week – figures which they felt completely justified the strategy of the speech. Most attention had focused on the drop in support for power-sharing among unionists. In the summer of 1998 well over 70 per cent of unionists supported power-sharing, now apparently 56 per cent are against, and hard-core unionist support for the agreement is down to 32.9 per cent. But there are other, more subtle, messages contained in the poll's findings.

Dublin has been increasingly interested in the notion that Peter Robinson was the new coming force in unionist politics. Mr Robinson has been saying interesting things. His public remarks have been widely interpreted as signalling the necessity for a DUP-Sinn Féin understanding as the way forward in Northern Ireland. How credible is Mr Robinson and his alleged project? Mr Robinson, it appears, has a popularity rating of only 7 per cent among unionists and is the deputy leader of a party only 2.7 per cent of whose supporters back power-sharing with the SDLP and Sinn Féin. In the light of these figures, the wager on Mr Robinson seems a very risky one. Mr Trimble remains, however, the most popular unionist leader (just edging out Dr Paisley) whilst his party's supporters in the country are ten times more likely to support power-sharing with the SDLP and Sinn Féin.

Mr Blair's spin doctors made sure that the media's attention was drawn to the sections of the speech that sent a clear message to the republican movement. In particular, they flagged his explicit reference to the fact that he could no longer expect the citizens of Belfast to accept Sinn Féin in government whilst the Dublin government was saying that Sinn Féin's participation in the government for the Republic required IRA disbandment.

Even so, some unionists were irritated by the tone of the speech. It was not just the green-tinted version of history that Mr Blair advanced – after all, there is nothing new in the British establishment's rather intellectually lazy embrace of the simpler nationalist versions of Irish history. Rather, what alarmed unionist sceptics was the talk of further implementation of the agreement and further guarantees to republicans.

For most unionists, the agreement has already been implemented fully on their side. There is still, of course, a debate about policing. But that cuts both ways. The agreement insists, above all, that Northern Ireland has a police service capable of enforcing public order; throughout the summer, the authorities were, in effect, saying that temporarily at least that was no longer the case.

Sinn Féin, however, is demanding that the British state abandon control of a police service for which it pays. It seems an unlikely prospect, and it is certainly not one heralded in the agreement.

But it may be that the real negotiation that Sinn Féin now has to have is with its own political aspirations. The British will always be willing to help by selling them, as so often, the same horse (in this case the agreement) twice. The message of Mr Blair's speech, however, is that Sinn Féin has a bright political future in the north, but this can only be achieved if the northern institutions are up and running. The northern institutions are now not likely to get up and running while the IRA remains active as a paramilitary force.

The republican leadership will be telling us all in the next few weeks about how they wish to engage with others and test their commitment to the Good Friday Agreement. In fact, the most profound engagement will be with the scale of their own ambitions. They have come a long way, and there is no sense in turning back now. For all its emollience, some of Mr Blair's language will not have made it easy for them. It is not so much the placing of blame at the door of the IRA. Republicans know better than anyone what really happened in Florida, Colombia, Castlereagh and Stormont, not to mention the recent arrests in the Republic – leading spectacularly, it is being said, to trials in four separate jurisdictions.

Rather, it was Mr Blair's explicit description of Stormont as a "partitionist assembly" and his reference to working with, not against, British security forces.

But the message of Ed Moloney's book, *The Secret History of the IRA*, is unambiguous. Mr Adams has enjoyed for some time a more complete control over the destiny of the republican movement than has been publicly acknowledged. For a time now he will have to engage in a little anger management with the grass roots. But he cannot afford to leave things as they are. A collapse of the institutions at a moment when the British government blamed the unionists contains certain advantages for the republican movement. A collapse which weakened David Trimble – the only unionist leader in a generation to have real credibility in British politics – also had potential advantages. But a collapse in which the British government blames the IRA and which leaves Mr Trimble the strongest leader in unionism contains no advantages.

So Mr Adams will be back with an offer. The IRA, we will soon hear, is part of the problem. The British government will have no difficulty in exerting increased pressure on the loyalist paramilitaries who have behaved so badly in recent months. But will it be enough for a sceptical unionist public opinion?

The latest poll catches a particular moment of sharp disillusionment with the experiment in power-sharing thus far. But Mr Trimble's continuing popularity with the electorate shows that not all is lost. One point should be noted, however. The political class in all the parties is more keen to resurrect Stormont than the unionist populace; when Stormont was actually functioning, both the UUP and DUP could take comfort from the fact that most of their supporters in the country – whatever their irritations with the agreement – did not want their party to be the first to withdraw from the assembly. This, indeed, was a powerful factor making for the survival of the institutions for as long as they did.

But now we are in a new situation which will require the generation of a new wave of optimism to allow the recreation of the institutions. Nothing short of the most dramatic and tangible activity by the IRA will suffice. Mr Adams has his work cut out.

ଔ ଔ ଔ

VICTORY FOR THE EXTREMES WILL DOOM THE BELFAST AGREEMENT
The Daily Telegraph, 22 April 2003

Why is the British government sleepwalking into an unnecessary election in Northern Ireland on May 29 – a contest that is likely to spell the end of the Belfast Agreement? Under the present circumstances, such an election would have only one conceivable outcome: dominant status inside each of the two communities for Sinn Féin and the anti-agreement Democratic Unionist Party led by Ian Paisley. The Northern Ireland peace process, presented by Tony Blair to George Bush as an exemplar of how to leave ancient hatreds behind, might soon be swept away by the victory of two parties whose *raison d'être* lies in harking back to past grievances.

It is worth recalling how we got here. Last October, the government suspended the Provincial Executive at Stormont after the discovery of an alleged republican spy ring at the heart of the Northern Ireland Office. Trust no longer obtained between unionists and nationalists. Since then, the British and Irish governments, with the help of the Americans, have been seeking to negotiate a package that would enable them to restore those institutions.

Until recent days, both states claimed to believe they were on the verge of negotiating a "historic" deal – whereby the IRA gave up paramilitary activity for good. The idea was that with such a deal in the bag, the pro-agreement Ulster Unionist Party, led by David Trimble, could face an assembly election in May in good heart. But now there is no deal, merely a debacle, with republicans signalling long, protracted negotiations ahead.

Worse still, the British and Irish governments appear willing to reward Sinn Féin for this intransigence by allowing assembly elections to proceed as if all were well. There are a number of short- and long-term reasons for the forward march of northern republicanism. Sinn Féin is younger, sharper and more dynamic than the ageing SDLP. It has also been the recipient of endless British concessions that have enabled it to portray the main constitutional nationalist party as a bunch of patsies who sold northern Catholics short. Thus, the SDLP took the risk of signing up to support the reformed Police Service of Northern Ireland, only to find that the British appeared to be willing to reform it further in order to win the support of republicans – which they still do not enjoy despite such concessions. What does it tell young Catholics when Sinn Féin misbehaves and is still rewarded?

Much the same applies on the other side of the sectarian divide. In reaction to such ethnic triumphalism and the apparent failure of the UUP to secure both devolution and an end to the IRA, the unionist majority might well also plump for the most hardline representatives of its communal interests in the shape of the DUP. Such a policy is very risky. But there is a school of thought in the highest reaches of the British state that holds that only a deal between the extremes is sustainable in the long run. It is a line of reasoning to which the Americans have also succumbed at times. According to this analysis, both the SDLP and the UUP are dispensable. The "moderates" have done their bit, forced both "extremes" to work within the parameters of the deal they constructed, and should now depart for the dustbin of history. Much better to have young republicans doing the policing, albeit roughly and readily, than bombing London.

Some mandarins felt a similar attraction to the prospect of DUP dominance. Much better, they reason, to have the disciplined DUP inside the tent: rhetorically sharp-edged, to be sure, but not susceptible to endless challenges from discontented hardliners after the fashion of the ill-disciplined UUP under Mr Trimble's leadership. This explains the vogue among certain officials in both states for Ian Paisley's deputy, Peter Robinson. Praising Mr Robinson even became an unlikely minor cottage industry among a certain breed of nationalist journalists.

The Robinson boomlet in Whitehall has subsided, either because Mr Robinson wanted no part of it or because he could not deliver what the governments wanted of him. But even if he was so inclined, circumstances would not now allow it. The DUP could only have pulled off such a trick if Mr Trimble had conducted a successful negotiation for some sort of end to the IRA campaign. This would inevitably involve some unionist concessions to make such a move palatable to the republican grassroots. The DUP could then have condemned Mr Trimble and all his works, and scooped up the big prizes at the expense of the "traitor". But because there has been no such deal, a victorious DUP would now have to engage in such a grubby negotiation itself – something it cannot do.

In other words, the British have kept on with a strategy – elections – that cannot yield anything good for them in the current, altered conditions. Again, there are a number of reasons for this, long-term and short-term. Tony Blair has, after all, almost lost the agreement once before, during the summer 1999. Distracted by the Kosovo war and its aftermath, he placed almost unbearable pressure on the pro-agreement unionists. Now, consumed by Iraq and for months fed an over-optimistic line by Dublin, he is about to repeat the mistake with irretrievable fatal consequences.

Above all, Mr Blair finds himself in this predicament because of his overly deferential approach to his Irish counterpart, Bertie Ahern. The Irish continue ill-advisedly to push for elections. The argument in Dublin has been that the IRA's move into constitutional politics has been bought by offering it political concessions. To suspend elections, the Fianna Fáil-led government argues, is to undermine the entire basis of the engagement with Sinn Féin of the past decade.

But what would we be holding elections to? After all, the circumstances that led to the suspension of Stormont last October still obtain. Without IRA disbandment and a promise from republicans that "the war is over", it would be impossible to recreate an inclusive provincial government. What, therefore, would be the purpose of holding an election to a body that could not possibly reconstitute itself as a viable executive for a very considerable time to come?

ᘓ ᘓ ᘓ

A PYRRHIC VICTORY IN THE POLLS: DIRECT RULE TINGED WITH GREEN
The Sunday Times, 30 November 2003

The British government is said to be shocked by the outcome of Wednesday's poll in Northern Ireland. It ought not to be. In the end, those who pressed for this election, whether in New York or Dublin, whether Sinn Féin or anti-agreement unionist, have had their victory, and a pyrrhic one it is.

The Paisleyite victory means that a vista of direct rule with a green tinge opens up for Northern Ireland. The DUP has a pragmatic and devolutionist element, but it is unlikely to gain the initiative any time soon.

A majority of DUP supporters in the country actively prefer direct rule to devolution. Paisley has already begun his campaign for Europe in June 2004. He will not permit any moves that will allow him to be embarrassed on that campaign trail.

Some pundits believe the threat of joint authority will bring the DUP to heel. The harsh truth is that most DUP supporters believe they are living under a form of joint authority already. The British government is anyway very wary of this form of governing.

There is, of course, the matter of the proposed review of the agreement. It is already being said by optimists that one man's review is another man's renegotiation. But this is simply not true. The review deals only with the efficiency and fairness of assembly procedures. It does not embrace those wider issues of north-south and east-west relations which the DUP has put on its shopping list.

Either the DUP radically moderates its attitude to the agreement or, indeed, Sinn Féin radically moderates its position. The review itself provides no way through – though it will be interesting to see how the DUP approaches it, given Paisley's objection to negotiation with Sinn Féin.

As the Belfast Agreement enters a crisis, and that is putting it kindly, it is tempting to ask about the might-have-beens. What if Richard Haass, President Bush's envoy, had not been precisely the Polyanna he always denied being? What if the British government had been able to maintain the quality of its early engagement?

In the week of Good Friday 1998, Tony Blair demonstrated an ability to look after pro-agreement unionism while keeping republicanism in tow. It was a surprising and sophisticated effort. In recent years, the quality of the British government's interventions has declined. The arid period of John Reid's spell as secretary of state was unique in that it did not have one single achievement to its name. This was the period when it was most obvious that corrective action, not mere rhetoric, was necessary to preserve pro-agreement unionism. Instead, one possible confidence-building measure such as the border poll (now ironically and belatedly demanded by the SDLP as well as the UUP) was rejected. Another, the international monitoring commission on paramilitary activity, was delayed so long as to render it valueless in this campaign.

Then there is the role of Dublin. Dublin has traditionally championed northern nationalism, while Britain has had a much more neutral attitude towards unionism. The resultant imbalance has always worried the Northern Ireland Office, particularly in the Peter Mandelson era, but in the end little was done to correct it.

There is no denying that the biggest problem with the implementation of the agreement lay in the failure of the republican movement to complete the transition from paramilitarism. It was this failure that allowed the leaders of anti-agreement unionism, who were on the back foot in the summer of 1998, to become the triumphant vote-grabbers in last week's election.

In a powerful House of Commons speech last month, Seamus Mallon acknowledged the damage done to unionist confidence by reports of IRA adventurism through the Florida arms case on to Colombia and the various alleged espionage scandals. In a telling phrase on Thursday, Peter Robinson claimed the Belfast agreement had died a year ago. The implication was clear. The Stormontgate crisis that brought about the suspension of the assembly had been a killer blow.

The prime minister's acts of completion speech at the Harbour Commissioners in October 2002 was a desperate attempt to retrieve the situation. But Tony Blair was perceived by unionists to have walked away from that speech when he called the November election while that agenda remained unfulfilled.

As long as the assembly was actually functioning, the devolutionist pragmatism of the DUP lieutenants was allowed expression because most ordinary DUP voters feared the consequences of actually withdrawing from the executive. But as soon as the executive was suspended – in a context in which their worst suspicion about the IRA was confirmed – unionist sentiment gravitated in a more hardline direction.

A renewed nationalist narrative that has deep legitimising roots in Irish historical experience is, however, now inevitable. Unionists will be said to have turned down the offer of equality in favour of the illusion of supremacy. David Trimble's remarkable poll-topping performance in Upper Bann implies that pro-agreement unionism was a viable project, that, even with the emergence of Sinn Féin as the largest nationalist party, the deal might just have been preserved. But as the voice of anti-agreement unionism becomes stronger, nationalists and republicans will ignore that thought in favour of a weary dismissal of the other community's story.

Some will say that an unnecessary complex and expensive form of government has gone and good riddance. It was always difficult to see how the assembly might function in the long term without a proper opposition. But there is reason to weep. Northern Ireland needs to displace its sectarian conflict into reasonably harmless disputes; this is for the most part what the institutions or the agreement did. Our politicians were never so happy when they spent hours in Stormont's myriad Byzantine committees. Some of the benign effects trickled down into society at large. Now there is no counterbalance to the working of mutual antagonism. We will be lucky not to feel the negative consequences.

CB CB CB

COLD REALISM STILL NEEDED IN ULSTER
Yorkshire Post, 10 December 2004

The British and Irish governments are still putting the best face on it. The Irish Prime Minister, banishing his initial pessimism, had joined the British Prime Minister in Belfast to insist that Northern Ireland was still on the verge of a historic "deal of deals" – the unity of the extremes of the unionist DUP party and Sinn Féin in a power-sharing government.

The two governments are entitled to claim significant progress. Both the DUP and Sinn Féin had agreed the broad outlines of a deal on political structures which then collapsed following a dispute over whether the IRA's promised disarmament should be photographed. Considering that the DUP leader Ian Paisley built his career in the 1970s on opposing this sort of deal, this is undoubted change in the longer perspective.

But the attempt to give a hugely positive spin to the recent negotiating collapse is obscuring some important areas of difficulty which remain. And we have to ask serious questions about the recent negotiating strategies of both the DUP and Sinn Féin.

It is necessary to protest against the naïve view of Paisleyism. The DUP and Sinn Féin have already shared power for 19 months in an executive.

Since 2002, the DUP leadership has been tacitly signalling its acceptance of the political structures of the Belfast Agreement, provided the governments arranged a few political fig leaves as they have here.

Ian Paisley is such a larger than life figure that his remarkable political guile is often underestimated. Like the prime minister, he is a brilliant actor. This week he allowed us to believe that he was hugely tempted by the prospect of becoming Northern Ireland's first minister.

Indeed, he probably is tempted. But it is clear from the denouement that he had two other, more important, pressing objectives in mind. The first was the public humiliation of the IRA as the only possible way of winning enough support in the Protestant community to support a new deal.

The polls – which in Northern Ireland usually overstate moderation – show that the bulk of DUP supporters do not, in principle, want a power-sharing deal with Sinn Féin. Paisley thinks that he can only deliver that deal if the IRA is made to look a supplicant.

This was not David Trimble's way of doing business. The Ulster Unionist Party leader and former first minister, even when he won a victory, accepted the prime minister's advice that rubbing the IRA's nose in it was a dangerous and counter-productive thing to do.

But we are now, for good or ill, on a new road. The question is: does the IRA's reduction in leverage, arising out of the reaction to 9/11, mean they have to accept lesser terms?

The argument over the photos, where the two governments and the IRA played into Paisley's hands, is merely a consequence of the DUP leader's understanding that the bulk of unionists need a firm adjudication against the IRA as the end note to the peace process.

The second Paisley objective was to delay any final deal until after the general election, in which he hopes to strengthen his party by eliminating all opposition within unionism.

But what about the Sinn Féin negotiating strategy? Did the leadership lean into accepting photographs only to be repulsed by middle management? Did they always want to delay a deal for reasons connected to their all-important and highly successful political strategy in the Republic of Ireland?

Certainly the governments continued to encourage a DUP hope that photographs were possible, long after there was any reasonable chance. Sinn Féin was, like the DUP, concerned to avoid the blame game here.

To pose these questions is a necessary corrective to the world of hype. The government papers published this week show issues of policing and justice – two big deal breakers – were still not resolved. While the IRA's new offer on decommissioning looks very promising, the rest of the language in the IRA's "new mode of existence" is no better than commitments already given to David Trimble in 2003.

The DUP publicly demanded this week that the IRA give the order to stand down. But where is that? And what is the status of the IRA's "green book", under which the IRA recruits and trains its volunteers? There may well be benign answers to all these questions, but they will now have to be answered before the final breakthrough is achieved.

Meanwhile, the mood in the bulk of the DUP is one of relief rather than disappointment. To argue for a greater realism is not to do the peace process a disservice. Quite the contrary. David

Trimble's brave and generous efforts were defeated in part by the over-eagerness of governments to gild the lily.

Governments have an understandable need to push the process on by looking on the bright side. But the prospect of a genuine deal, which is now surely possible, is better served by cold realism.

03 03 03

THE MURDER THAT HAS PUT THE WIND UP SINN FÉIN
The Daily Telegraph, 1 March 2005

Even after Sunday's protest over the IRA murder of Robert McCartney, Sinn Féin can draw upon intense emotions of loyalty in Northern Irish working-class Catholic neighbourhoods. Even McCartney's family have said that he was a Sinn Féin voter.

Sinn Féin, too, has a network of local activists who can deliver services to the population. These advantages will not disappear overnight. The SDLP, the party of moderate nationalism, now has a chance to avoid the electoral decimation that many felt was just around the corner – but we do not yet have sufficient evidence to suggest that it can again become the leading force within northern nationalism.

In the Irish Republic, things are very different. Last summer, Sin Féin enjoyed major successes in the local and European elections, but today the party is pilloried in headline after headline on the issue of criminality. There is a paradox here. Despite all subsequent rhetoric, neither the British nor the Irish government had a red line on crime issues in the negotiations which stretched from Leeds Castle in September to the pathetic debacle of the stillborn "comprehensive agreement" of 8 December. Their so-called anti-crime formula in Annexe C did not, for example, forbid cross-border smuggling or money-laundering. The IRA made it clear that it would not accept even the comparatively weak language committing it "not to endanger anyone's personal rights and safety".

While their great *bête noire* in Irish politics, Michael McDowell, the minister for justice – Gerry Adams once called him the "green Paisley" – now sets the agenda, Sinn Féin supporters take comfort from the fact that their poll ratings have remained solid in the current crisis. Even so, the personal rating of Gerry Adams has plummeted with voters in the Republic.

Sinn Féin cadres regard this as the leader taking a necessary hit for the party; they remain confident that their electoral potential remains solid, but they may be wrong to be quite so sanguine. In the last general election, the brand image of Mr Adams was central to the party's advance. If that image is tarnished, is it conceivable that the party will continue its upward momentum? Sinn Féin may retain a solid base of support but be treated as a pariah by other parties – such a loss of respectability is a serious blow in the coalition politics of the Irish Republic.

This brings us to a deeper problem. Sinn Féin's appeal in the south has been based on its appropriation of the story of Ireland and Irish patriotism and on its image as crimefighter by any means necessary. Republicans have sauntered across the stage of Irish politics since 1998 like returning war heroes. They, after all, fought the British for 25 years – 1969-94 – while Mr Ahern's political ancestors in the Old IRA only did it for three years: Ahern's father fought the British from 1918-21. They were legitimated by a popular version of history, which blamed Britain and the Ulster Protestants for Ireland's woes. Mr Adams was among the most famous Irishmen on the planet – in particular, he was more popular than Bertie Ahern among Irish-Americans. Sinn Féin was not implicated in the obesely bourgeois corruption of the Dublin political scene. The new allegations about money-laundering, the licensing of Dublin criminals and shady dealings in corporate high finance are a challenge to the purity of Sinn Féin's self-image.

Above all, the republican leaders were engaged in an audacious attempt to transform the traditional relationship between northern and southern nationalism. For most of the nineteenth and twentieth centuries, northern nationalists accepted a subordinate role, while the leadership was granted to southerners. This generation of republicans was determined to end all that and bring the leadership north. To do this, they ruthlessly exploited the ambiguities of the peace process.

Sinn Féin was both a system and an anti-system party linked to the IRA and not linked to the IRA. Criticisms of Sinn Féin were muted because of its alleged implications for the northern peace process: instead, the Irish government colluded with the British in the destruction of the centre ground in the north.

John Bruton, the former Irish prime minister and current European ambassador in Washington, was seen to be damaged because he could be described by political opponents as "John Unionist". Both the Michael Collins movie, which had an enormous impact in Ireland, and the bicentenary commemorations of the 1798 rising enhanced the credibility of Sinn Féin. The success of the "Celtic Tiger" in some ways revived a more self-confident chauvinist nationalism, which Sinn Féin exploited.

But all this positive Sinn Féin momentum is now placed in jeopardy. Tony Blair has very recently made it clear that he regards the Good Friday Agreement as his greatest achievement in politics. That agreement was always a brave gamble against the odds.

However, with the air thick with IRA threats of a return to violence, the prime minister faces the prospect that not only will he lose the agreement, but that he will also lose it in the worst possible way.

As with Harold Wilson before him, his indulgence of the IRA is infuriating substantial sections of respectable Middle Ireland. Understandably, he continues to dream fitfully of one more attempt at a Sinn Féin -DUP deal.

So does Sinn Féin, anxious to restore some of its lost respectability. So, too, does a section of the DUP which had, after all, accepted the revival of the Good Friday Agreement plus the devolution of policing and justice last November.

And might the impossible happen? Some massive IRA concession to resurrect the peace process? There's a chance, but I wouldn't bet my house on it.

ೞ ೞ ೞ

IS IT REALLY THE END OF THE IRA?
Yorkshire Post, 29 July 2005

Did *The Sun* newspaper get it right? Following some powerful Downing Street spin, we were told yesterday that the IRA was about to surrender. The IRA was not only going to end its paramilitary activity, but also end recruitment.

This raised eyebrows. Back in 1998, in the Prime Minister's final pitch for the Good Friday Agreement, Tony Blair told the people of Northern Ireland that Sinn Féin could not be in government unless the IRA ended recruitment.

But, for some years now, the government has dropped this demand. Instead, it has focused on other issues such as arms importation. It would have been remarkable indeed if a return to virtue on this scale was anticipated. This is a significant matter. Because if the IRA, though not disbanded, is now just an "old boys club", why would it need to go on recruiting young fellows?

But when the IRA statement of future intent finally came, by DVD, it was silent on this matter, with Tony Blair reduced to interpreting the announcement as meeting the government's demands on paramilitarism and criminality.

The key sentences in the IRA statement run as follows: "All volunteers have been instructed to assist the development of purely political and democratic programmes through exclusively peaceful means. Volunteers must not engage in any other activities whatsoever." But what is the IRA's definition of a peaceful activity? Could it possibly include its lucrative smuggling trade?

At this point the truth is that there is still ambiguity, and we do not actually know. That is why the White House was right to declare that the statement was potentially historic.

Nonetheless, Mr Blair has reason to be proud of yesterday's work. Worried Londoners can feel a trifle less worried about their personal security. Let us not forget that only a few months ago the IRA issued two statements talking about the transience of the peace process which were basically threats. Mr Blair is entitled to feel that he has now moved the IRA to a much more benign place, and that the London police will not be faced with a war on two fronts.

"England's difficulty is Ireland's opportunity" is one of the great clichés of Irish nationalist thought. In fact, it has very rarely proved to be the case. But there are still those concerned with the safety and security of the British state who lie awake at night worrying about the possibility of a war on two fronts, given al-Qaeda's recent bombings in London. From that point of view, yesterday's events were an unalloyed triumph.

But matters in Northern Ireland are more complex. Many unionists have long felt that the IRA's traditional armed campaign was over. Since 9/11, it was politically impossible for the IRA to bomb London again and retain any degree of support in the United States.

The unionist concern in Northern Ireland, shared by a significant number of constitutional nationalists north and south, is that taking Sinn Féin into government opens the way to a Mafia state.

What is the strategy of Gerry Adams here? Bluntly, it is to regain the initiative for the republican movement. In the wake of recent scandals, Sinn Féin's advance in the Republic of Ireland has stalled. Mr Adams' own personal rating – the key to their advance – has dropped. This is due to some unfortunate reminders that

Sinn Féin's continuing violent and criminal activity after the IRA ceasefire can affect the Republic, too.

But nothing is more soothing to the population of the Republic of Ireland than the reappearance of Mr Adams at a press conference, reassuring everyone once more that they have nothing to fear from the IRA. Ideally, for Mr Adams the new move will put pressure on the Reverend Ian Paisley's Democratic Unionist Party to form a government in Northern Ireland with Sinn Féin. Even if the DUP continues to reject such a deal, Sinn Féin reckons to pocket concessions from the British government on demilitarisation and other issues. The release of Sean Kelly – the Shankill Road bomber only recently declared a danger to public order – is a dramatic indication of this.

Of course, the release of Kelly infuriates unionist politicians, as did Mr Blair's unfortunate remarks last week, drawing a benign distinction between the IRA and al-Qaeda. But, at the moment, Mr Blair can afford to offend unionist opinion, because the mood of the unionist community only becomes important several months from now.

The Irish government hopes that it has persuaded Dr Paisley that a mere six months will be long enough to judge the sincerity of the IRA's intentions. There are those in the British government who share this hope and tell us that, in private, Dr Paisley is much more moderate than he appears in public. Underlining all this is one basic question rather neglected in yesterday's flurry of events.

The final resolution of this process requires republican acceptance of policing in Northern Ireland. Sinn Féin sees this as involving Sinn Féin control of either the new devolved Ministry of Policing or Justice. On the basis of a settlement in which the IRA has not disbanded, is the DUP ready for that accommodation? The signs yesterday, on balance, are that the DUP wants to hang tough.

But one certainty can be gleaned from yesterday's events. Historic or otherwise, the IRA statement simply opens the door to more "process" in Northern Ireland.

CB CB CB

TEST OF WILLS AS PRESSURE NOW GROWS ON DUP TO ACT
Irish Independent, 27 September 2005

There was no anti-climax. The IRA has dumped arms as promised. Gerry Adams is not going to be the Irish Ho Chi Minh, expelling the foreign invader following a Hibernian-style Tet Offensive. Indeed, it requires an effort of will to recall that this was the concept which underpinned the mass smuggling of arms from Colonel Gaddafi in the mid-1980s.

The two governments are ecstatic as promised, but what about the DUP? How will Dr Paisley's party react to recent events? How soon will they be compelled to treat Sinn Féin as a party just like the others?

There are two ways of looking at the most recent phase of the peace process, and there are two possible interpretations. The first suggests that, with the Northern Bank robbery and the McCartney murder, the IRA overplayed its hand. Irish America got very angry indeed. Bertie Ahern and Tony Blair were also rather annoyed. The pressure then built upon Gerry Adams to turn things around by a dramatic new initiative. As a result of the pressure exerted from the three governments the IRA has decided to go out of business.

That is the benign view. Here is another view considerably less benign. It points out that in the negotiations which stretched through Leeds Castle to December 8, 2004, the Sinn Féin leadership made the revealing strategic decision to prioritise the "amour propre" of the IRA over the need to protect the Good Friday

Agreement from DUP efforts to renegotiate it. It was a remarkable moment.

Nationalist Ireland would have been highly supportive of any party which stood militantly by the text and spirit of the Good Friday Agreement. That is not the route the republican leadership chose. Sinn Féin permitted the DUP to negotiate a symbolic reduction in the partnership nature of the agreement. It allowed the SDLP to gain traction as true defenders of the agreement – a development which saved the SDLP from electoral meltdown in the North.

On the other hand, the republican leadership refused to give way on the issue of a photograph of IRA decommissioning or, indeed, the explicit language on an end to criminality and intimidation demanded by the two governments.

We are now asked to believe that the IRA, which was so important to the Sinn Féin leadership a few months ago, has been placed in the dustbin of history. For example, the two governments "expect" that it has stopped recruiting, and an organisation which no longer recruits new members is clearly a dying organisation. It may be so. But the other way of looking at these events, somewhat less flattering to the two governments, is that the Sinn Féin leadership sensed their fear at the impending collapse of the whole agreement project and ruthlessly exploited it. The British and Irish governments then made a decision to place the heaviest political burden of sustaining the process on the DUP in much the same way as they used to do with David Trimble. The three governments who supported the DUP's demand for photographic evidence of decommissioning have left the DUP in the lurch.

The DUP, insofar as it was tempted last year by a deal, was tempted on the basis that it could claim vastly better terms than David Trimble. Indeed, that they could claim that the photograph of IRA decommissioning constituted a justified humiliation and was therefore the greatest Protestant victory since 1690. Sops will come, but the DUP is left with no aesthetic of victory left, no grand narrative.

It has therefore only one alternative, which is to stick it out and to play for time. They made a reasonable fist yesterday of exploiting some of the ambiguities in the General's press conference. A policy of delay might be disappointing to some of the Young Turks in the DUP, but doing otherwise would be to fly in the face of their electoral base. When and if the talks ever restart, they will confront another difficulty. Since December the DUP has extended its agenda against the Good Friday Agreement. This makes the Irish government in particular very nervous. Further changes would be very hard to concede.

But the DUP has openly campaigned for further changes to the agreement, including the end to the D'Hondt system and the turning of the first minister into a real prime minister and not a deputy co-premiership with the deputy first minister.

Yesterday's euphoria should not hide the fact that these negotiations, if and when they open, will be a messy business. But behind all this lies the biggest question of all. Is a DUP/Sinn Féin government in the North the best route to stability of the island of Ireland, still less the world class society and world class economy which Peter Hain claims Northern Ireland needs to fend off the threat of an increasingly competitive international capitalist market?

03 03 03

SHADOWY ALLIANCE HAUNTS STORMONTGATE
Yorkshire Post, 22 December 2005

What on earth is going on in the latest phase of the so-called Stormontgate saga? In October 2002, the government announced that it had uncovered an IRA spy ring at the heart of the Northern Ireland Office and the devolved institutions. Highly sensitive documents – including conversations between President

Bush and Tony Blair – were discovered in republican West Belfast.

Up to a few days ago, it was confidently assumed that three people were to face charges in court in this connection. Then it was announced that it was not in the public interest to carry on with the trial and the three defendants were found not guilty, with no stain on their character.

Sinn Féin was delighted, as it had denied all along that there had been any spy ring. Then Denis Donaldson – whose relationship to Gerry Adams is similar to that of Downing Street chief-of-staff Jonathan Powell to Tony Blair – outed himself as a 20-year-long British spy. Sinn Féin immediately got out its narrative, and sections of the media gave it credibility.

Mr Adams insisted that this was further proof that the spy ring had never existed and that the whole affair had been got up by so-called securocrats – senior officials in the Northern Ireland Office and elsewhere, who were working to undermine Tony Blair's agenda.

But is this even remotely likely? In the first place, those whom Sinn Féin named as securocrats gave every sign of being inconvenienced by the Stormontgate affair. It was their job, after all, to deliver the institutions of the Good Friday Agreement and to keep Mr Adams locked into the peace process. In that sense, there has been, for many years now, a profound commonality of interest between the British security establishment and Mr Adams.

Far from launching the Stormontgate affair to "save Dave" – to give then Ulster Unionist leader David Trimble an excuse to walk away from power-sharing – the securocrats took the view that Mr Trimble should ignore the spying scandal and stay in government with Sinn Féin. Today they take exactly the same view: that this current unfortunate incident should be forgotten about.

In the last couple of days the Sinn Féin narrative has begun to crumble, to be replaced by another question: how many more agents are there in the republican leadership and what does this say about an agenda of tacit co-operation with the British state?

This, after all, is historically how Britain achieves peace in Ireland. In 1920-21, the police and army regularly made raids on leading Sinn Féin figures, only to discover that they were under the protection of other parts of the British state. Those arrested were rapidly released even when incriminating material was found; in one famous case, that of Erskine Childers in 1921, a senior British official carried his bags out of jail.

What is the political fall-out? The government continues to be optimistic about devolution, although it appears to be publicly assuming that it will not happen in 2006.

There is an element of rationalisation in this. Neither British nor Irish governments can afford to say that they were handed a political miracle – the Good Friday Agreement – and bungled it. The Prime Minister is widely perceived to be in the grip of "legacy-itis" in Northern Ireland, and though he may not have noticed this, the local population certainly has.

The row over Stormontgate has intensified the lack of trust between the two communities. Unionists feel that the IRA still thinks it can get away with lying to them, as with the bank robbery. Emotions of anger on this score have now been sharply revived. On the other hand, many nationalists believe that wicked British spies have perpetrated yet another offence against decent Irish patriots.

The point to note is that the current political agenda contains two issues: the amnesty-type proposals for the republicans' so-called "on-the-runs" and, more importantly, the issue of restorative justice which the SDLP sees as British government willingness to hand the "hood" over to the "hoods", which will continue to poison the debate well into 2006.

Into this mix, the government plans to devolve policing and justice and thus enhance Sinn Féin's power in this highly sensitive sphere. It is, in fact, possible, however, that Mr Blair is more realistic about Northern Ireland policy than Secretary of State Peter Hain and the Northern Ireland Office can afford to be. Mr Blair may, in his heart of hearts, have grave doubts about the DUP's capacity to do a deal that is worthwhile. He may even believe that he has, in effect, achieved his Northern Ireland work by the "defanging" of the republican movement.

If devolution comes, it would be a bonus, but the big objective of British policy has already been achieved, and there is always the possibility of an Anglo-Irish Agreement mark two to complete the Northern Irish political settlement. This does, however, leave a problem for Peter Hain, a naturally ambitious politician.

Paul Murphy's recent removal broke the rule of thumb whereby every Northern Ireland Secretary who was not actually retiring moved on to another Cabinet position, usually a promotion, as a reward for a hardship stint.

Mr Hain was brought in to provide an activist contrast to Mr Murphy's genuine decency and more measured and cautious approach. He has certainly provided the contrast, but with a conspicuous lack of success. He must be worrying that the Prime Minister has landed him with an impossible task and that he will personally take the rap for failure.

03 03 03

A Man in a Hurry – A Man in no Hurry
Parliamentary Brief, October 2006

The official line of the British and Irish governments is that "it's all to play for". They have announced that the Northern Irish parties will be invited to St Andrews some time in October for yet another negotiation to bring about that elusive Sinn Féin–DUP deal. But the truth is that there is very little chance of re-establishing the Good Friday Agreement institutions by the November deadline. Failure to do so, both governments say, will open up a new era in Northern Irish politics, dominated by increased Anglo-Irish co-operation and an end at attempts to revive devolution until after the next British general election.

The problem for the governments is that this threat has little leverage on the DUP or the unionist community more generally. Unionists are broadly of two types: those who believe they have been living under Anglo-Irish joint authority for 20 years, and those who have little problem with an Irish government role in the North, especially now the irredentist articles 2 and 3 of the Irish constitution have gone. It is not clear how the governments' "threat" has leverage with either constituency.

The governments will be able to point to increasingly ecstatic reports from the International Monitoring Commission and, indeed, the way in which the Preparation for Government Committee in the assembly, after a wretched start, has been doing some good work.

In fact, there is still some possibility of a November deal – though even the DUP "modernisers" have long looked to pencilling in something for next May. DUP leader Ian Paisley insists on full and intense Provo support for policing as the price of entering government, and refuses to contemplate devolution of policing and justice powers in the near future. Sinn Féin insists that it can only support policing when it has obtained devolution of policing and justice.

If Sinn Féin and the DUP retain their formal positions on policing there cannot be a deal. But there are clear signs of a public flexibility on both sides: Sinn Féin openly hint of further movement and Gregory Campbell of the DUP has called for "repentant" former paramilitaries to be admitted to the police service. There is an interesting dialogue taking place, in which DUP modernisers send signals to Sinn Féin and vice versa.

Sinn Féin, after all, is pretty desperate. The newspaper *Daily Ireland*, a huge drain on the finances of the movement, has folded – a setback for both morale and strategy. It is one of many disappointments for Sinn Féin, and some experts are now moving their electoral projections downward – predicting ten seats for the party after the next Irish election. A decent performance for a normal party, but a poor return on a revolutionary messianic project.

Worse still, there is no guarantee that the party will return to government in the North next year. The only factor which might lift Sinn Féin's electoral credibility in the South is a return to government in the North.

They are fortunate, perhaps, in that the DUP itself does not seem to care one way or another about Sinn Féin's strength in the Irish parliament. For Sinn Féin on the other hand, the driving imperative of policy is to return to government in the North before the next Irish election in order to increase their respectability with a nervous Irish electorate.

Sinn Féin needs to start winning the battle of the headlines again; that is why Gerry Adams took the risk of alienating the US government by his recent Hamas trip: it is now more important for Mr Adams to win votes in the Republic than to retain Washington's support. We can expect, then, a big effort to forge a deeper understanding, with the DUP modernisers, but even the DUP modernisers freely acknowledge that public opinion in their community remains sceptical.

In part this is down to a mistake made by the British government. By refusing to press Sinn Féin hard on policing and instead implying that the DUP alone is the obstacle to a return to devolution it is sending out the wrong signals. Ordinary unionists detect that once again Sinn Féin is in the driving seat, and this is a bad omen for how a devolved government might work. This is particularly important because it undermines the DUP claims to have reversed the political terms of trade of the Trimble era.

But while Adams and Co. look increasingly ponderous, it should not be seen simply as a function of age, even if Adams has been around as leader twice as long as Tony Blair. After all, the leader who has a renewed resonance within Northern Ireland is the oldest MP: more and more Protestants, for so long critical and bitterly resentful of Dr Paisley, quietly support his current stand.

He has a popular appeal which is simply not enjoyed by the DUP modernisers. He has had one great advantage denied to David Trimble: on Paisley's watch, people began belatedly to believe that the Provos were not going back to war. As even Peter Hain has conceded, it is possible to have peace without devolution.

A policy of delay and caution in such a context has become remarkably attractive. There is no pent-up demand for devolution – expertly tapped into by David Trimble in 1998. Rather, the population is agnostic: they might still vaguely prefer devolution, but they know that it had no magical answer to the problems of the province.

The DUP has now publicly signalled its scepticism about doing a deal with Tony Blair. Nigel Dodds has said that the prime minister cannot now sell anything in Northern Ireland and Dr Paisley has echoed that concern.

November, then, is an unlikely date for the return of devolution: next summer is more likely, but it is worth noting that Peter Hain's suggestion of a deal after the next British general election is the one which would unify the DUP. But how long can the Adams leadership afford to wait? If he does not want to wait he has to move on policing.

ଓ ଓ ଓ

AESTHETICALLY UNAPPEALING BUT A VICTORY FOR LONDON AND DUBLIN
Sunday Independent, 18 March 2007

The people of Northern Ireland are on the verge of making a profound act of self-definition. They are close to accepting Ian Paisley and Martin McGuinness as the partners in the co-premiership set up under the Good Friday Agreement. At the Ballymena count on Wednesday, both Paisley and McGuinness purred with satisfaction as the results showed that they had vanquished their internal foes. The usual bouts of rhetoric aside, the mood was one of preparation for shared government.

For some, it was the most progressive moment in Ballymena since that day on 7 July 1798, when the United Irishmen seized the town, crying "Ballymena's our own – up with the Green and down with King Geordie", and established a Committee of Public Safety to lock up loyalist remnants. This time, at least, the victors were prepared to allow their enemies to lie, as Paisley put it, "under a pile of lost deposits". Others were less sanguine. The defeated activists of the SDLP and the Ulster Unionist Party were muttering about the triumph of the extremes and insisting a new government, based on the most visceral and atavistic factions of the Troubles, would be brutal, nasty and short.

We need to stop and take a breath for a moment. This week, Senator George Mitchell, the distinguished chairman of the Good Friday Agreement negotiations, insisted – almost certainly correctly – that the return of devolution is inevitable. In his memoir of the negotiation of the Good Friday Agreement, Senator Mitchell insisted – equally correctly – that only Ian Paisley's tactical error in walking out of the talks in 1997 had allowed David Trimble the space necessary to negotiate his part of the Good Friday Agreement. Now it is Paisley who will inherit the first minister's position – once held by Trimble – and, of course, the agreement which Trimble negotiated (with the addition of a few fig leaves).

The British government insists that all will be well. British officials acknowledge that neither the DUP nor Sinn Féin are exactly focussed on reconciliation, but they believe that the power-sharing structures of the Good Friday Agreement are so strong that they will have no alternative to compromise, in a dictatorship of political correctness presided over by the province's leading ethnic warriors. The Northern Ireland Office even believes that the Ulster Unionists and the SDLP failed to co-operate effectively because they were always being undermined by Paisley and Adams respectively. This time, at least, that problem has gone away.

There is some inter-governmental concern as to whether Dr Paisley realises that he is not going to be the prime minister of Northern Ireland in the way that Craigavon or Brookeborough were, but rather locked into a political cohabitation with Mr McGuinness, who has an equal status. Does he know the truth, officials worry? But in the main, the governments believe – not without reason – that Dr Paisley and Mr McGuinness have mellowed, and the new arrangements will work satisfactorily. They will have taken encouragement from Mr McGuinness's tone on Thursday, when he moved away from the talk of both Mr Adams and Dr Paisley, who have, in recent days, been projecting a battle a day. Mr McGuinness talked instead of mutual back-scratching. The outcome may be a little unsavoury for some sensitive souls, but it is, after all, what the people of Northern Ireland voted for.

This is, of course, true, but they voted in a particular context, determined by inter-governmental policy, which prioritised the survival of the Adams leadership over everything else. As late as 2005, the IRA publicly threatened a return to war, proof that it perceived that such a threat – long after 9/11, long after Omagh – was taken seriously by both governments. The result was the marginalisation of the SDLP in the 2001 Westminster general election and the Ulster Unionists in the 2003 Assembly elections. The insurance policy for the governments lay in the belief that the DUP's opposition to the Belfast Agreement was always more rhetorical than substantive. The outcome may be aesthetically unappealing, but it is a triumph for London and Dublin.

Will the deal be done by 26 March? The DUP lieutenants are giving the impression that there will be a delay and that there is tough negotiating ahead. In fact, their leverage with the Treasury has already gone. Now that Paisley has overcome his dissidents, what need of further bribes? Their leverage on policing is also reduced. The US State Department, which took a tougher line on this than the British or Irish governments, is now likely to say that, in the light of Mr Adams' decisive move, it is time for the DUP to reciprocate. Any St Patrick's Day events in Washington will be dominated by talk of the need for completion. If the DUP is serious, as its election manifesto suggests, about disbanding IRA paramilitary structures, this cannot be achieved in any short period of time. It is, however, more likely that further moves by the Provisionals on the policing issue will be taken as proof of the said dismantlement. It may take some time for all this to play out, and both Mr Adams (with the Irish election in mind) and Mr Blair (with his legacy in mind) can afford to wait a few weeks.

CB CB CB

VOTE FOR ME AND I'LL KEEP *HIM* IN ORDER
Parliamentary Brief, April 2007

Six months ago, on the eve of the St Andrews negotiation of October 2006, I argued in *Parliamentary Brief* that the impossible – a deal between Sinn Féin and the DUP – was now no longer that. The reason: that Adams, struggling in the Irish Republic opinion polls, needed the boost of entry into a power-sharing government in the north before the Republic's June 2007 election.

In such a context, he seemed likely to move the republican movement towards an acceptance of policing. In response, the DUP would be able to claim an effective end to IRA paramilitarism and move to cut the deal.

In effect, this is what happened at St Andrews and in the months following, albeit in a rather messy fashion. In the aftermath of the St Andrews agreement, the British and Irish governments appeared to have an open mind on whether to hold a referendum on a new deal or an election. The mandarins who favoured an election rather than a referendum won the debate.

It has to be said that in the short term at least, they have turned out to be right. Polling at the time suggested that St Andrews had not caught the public's imagination and, in particular, the imagination of the unionist community. A result like the 71 per cent Yes vote achieved for the Good Friday Agreement in 1998 seemed improbable in the absence of a similar mood for a historic compromise.

Instead, the governments allowed Sinn Féin and the DUP to mobilise around a different issue – who would be first minister, Ian Paisley or Martin McGuinness? The rules for the operation of the electoral college in the assembly, which would elect the first minister, were changed in order to enhance the possibility that it could go to either man. Both Paisley and McGuinness were given the perfect tribal rallying cry – stop the other tribe's leader.

The DUP were facilitated in another way. The St Andrews agreement demanded an explicit commitment to enter into a power-sharing executive on 26 March 2007. However, the party was allowed to evade that commitment, because the government rightly believed that Paisley wanted to do the deal and an electoral victory would strengthen his hand.

The DUP was able to campaign on both sides of the street, hinting to one constituency that it would do a deal, whilst seeking the support of others who still believed that the deal would never happen. It was a brilliant campaign. Ironically, only in Dr Paisley's North Antrim heartland were unionist anti-agreement dissidents strong enough to deny the DUP an extra seat.

Some commentators have rightly stressed the good performance of the moderate Alliance party and some signs of cross-community voting. Nonetheless, the big story of the election is the way in which tribal sectarian loyalty to perceived strong leadership has trumped every other issue.

Although both parties were set on a power-sharing compromise, remarkably neither Gerry Adams nor Ian Paisley had to concern themselves with questions about what the last 30 years of their non-compromising leaderships had been all about. Paisley mobilised on the basis that a strong hand would be necessary to deal with Sinn Féin and the Irish government. Adams mobilised on the basis that only Sinn Féin could seriously upset the Paisleyites.

The Ulster Unionist Party's poor performance was widely predicted. In fact, the party did at least well enough to end up with 18 seats, giving it a call on two ministerial positions in the new executive. Without David Trimble, they lost votes to the Alliance party in Belfast and to the DUP elsewhere.

The real surprise was the poor performance of the SDLP, leaving it with only one ministerial position in the new executive. Unlike the UUP, the SDLP had a better than expected general election in 2005.

Since then, the party has set the agenda in a striking way: on the "on the runs" issue, community restorative justice and the role of MI5. The SDLP often made the Sinn Féin leadership look slow and unreactive. These were all issues which, in principle, highlighted the moral story of democratic nationalism against the physical force tradition. Yet, when push came to shove, it did not matter. The electorate decided instead that Sinn Féin was the best force to challenge the other side.

These are bitter times for the centre parties who did so much to bring about the Good Friday Agreement. Peter Mandelson's revelations in the *Guardian* on 13 March 2007 recalled how the Provos were allowed to dominate the negotiations at the expense of all other parties in 2001.

Seamus Mallon, who shared the co-premiership of Northern Ireland with David Trimble at that time, suggested that Downing Street had a deliberate policy of undermining the centre and working towards a DUP-Sinn Féin deal. In fact, this may be a little unfair. Certainly, as far as the marginalisation of the UUP was concerned, Downing Street tended to believe that David Trimble could survive indefinitely. In the end, when Trimble's defeat came in November 2003, it was by a relatively small margin.

Within the governmental system, Mr Blair was the last to believe that the DUP could deliver power-sharing with Sinn Féin. He may well have intuited that those in the American, Irish and British governments who have supported the DUP option since 2002 tend to be long-termists prepared to wait for Peter Robinson as Dr Paisley's successor, and less than worried if this does not happen on Tony's watch.

The prime minister has probably lucked out now; but it is not the function of a long drawn out plot on his part and that, at least, is to his credit.

ଓ ଓ ଓ

THE POLITICAL FUTURE OF NORTHERN IRELAND: MODEL FOR WORLD PEACE OR HITLER-STALIN PACT, ULSTER-STYLE?
Frankfurter Allgemeine Sonntagszeitung, 1 April 2007

This week's power-sharing deal between Sinn Féin and Ian Paisley's Democratic Unionist Party marks the end of an era in the Ulster Troubles. These Troubles took the lives of 3,700 people in a province of only one and a half million. Hardly a family remained unscarred in the sense that everyone knew someone who had either been murdered or injured in the Troubles. The jackal's share of the killing was carried out by the IRA and its allies – almost 60 per cent – but 30 per cent were killed by Protestant militants and 10 per cent fell at the hands of security forces. The much-maligned police force killed 52 but suffered the loss of 302. The latest political deal is a further barrier against a return of these miseries, but it remains the case that the IRA has not killed a member of the Crown Forces in Ireland since 1997. In effect, the negotiation of the Good Friday Agreement in 1998 brought an end to mainstream Republican paramilitarism and loyalist violence has been dwindling markedly in recent times. So why then is this week's deal considered to be so epoch-making?

The French Marxist structuralists of the 1970s used to speak about the "problematic" of a discourse, by which they meant the system of questions and answers which governed that discourse. This idea helps us to see that the discourse of the peace process as we have seen it since the early 1990s is now concluded. This peace process began with the decision of the governments to bring the extremes of the conflict onto the political centre stage – firstly through a process of dangerous and secret dialogue. The new strategy was publicly announced in the Downing Street Declaration of 1993.

It offered Sinn Féin a role in the political future of Northern Ireland, provided that it permanently renounced violence. Both governments insisted that this permanent renunciation would be proven by the decommissioning of IRA weapons. Dr. Paisley correctly predicted that Sinn Féin would be included in talks about the future of Northern Ireland without the decommissioning of weapons. In fact, they were included in the government of Northern Ireland without that prior decommissioning. It was the correct nature of this prediction which fuelled Paisley's rise at the expense of David Trimble, the moderate Ulster Unionist leader who was trying to negotiate a compromise with Sinn Féin (the political leadership of the IRA). On the other hand, Paisley was wrong to say that the IRA would never decommission. They began that process for David Trimble in 2001-3 and finished it for Ian Paisley in 2005. More profoundly, Paisley was wrong in his view that it was impossible to negotiate political structures of power-sharing in the Good Friday Agreement mode which a majority of Unionists might regard as at least viable in principle. In fact, Paisley's acceptance of the framework negotiated by Trimble constitutes a politically-posthumous triumph for the Nobel Prize winner.

The fact remains that since the Downing Street Declaration certain questions have dominated the political field. Were the unionists up for power-sharing with Sinn Féin? Would the IRA decommission and support policing? This phase appears to be over.

We now apparently have affirmative answers to all these questions.

There is also a dark side – the marginalisation of those mainstream parties who took the early risks for peace and who were the least ideologically responsible for militancy. Was the collapse of the centre ground inevitable? Seamus Mallon, the former moderate nationalist leader who shared the co-premiership of Northern Ireland from 1998 to 2001, has argued that the Blair government pursued a deliberate policy of weakening the centre ground in order to enhance its deal with the extremes. This is probably unfair to Mr. Blair. He was genuinely dismayed when David Trimble crashed in 2003. Mr. Blair could point out that as early as 1998 the demographic trends were negative for the centre parties. The fact remains that for long after 9/11 the British Government behaved as if it believed that the IRA had a realistic option of returning to war. In consequence, it prioritised the needs of that faction over all others in Northern Ireland. The real fear was probably not of a sustained campaign, but of incidents like the Canary Wharf bomb of 1996; incidents which would have had great capacity to embarrass a government which had released all IRA prisoners. Those who today sing the praises of dialogue with terrorists should note that, while it can work, it also brings great risks and the price is usually paid by men of peace.

What is the future for Northern Ireland? Some say it already is a Hitler-Stalin Pact, Ulster-style; that this coalition of the extremes will inevitably usher in greater nastiness. It is certainly worrying that some of the provision for reconciliation in the Good Friday Agreement has been removed – for example, the requirement that the first and deputy first ministers should be elected with explicitly-granted cross-community support. On the other hand, others argue that the power-sharing rules involving compromise are so strong that the new system will work in a reasonably humane way. No-one can be sure, but what is clear is that it is not the end of history in Ireland, that the strategic battle between nationalism and unionism will continue. It is clear also that it is difficult to make this case a model for other conflict situations such as the Middle East. This is the first war in history in which one government – the British – has paid for the upkeep of the families of both sides. It is more a story of how difficult it is for a liberal democratic state to deal with terrorism within its own society, especially when it is encumbered by a sense of historic guilt, as the British state is about its role in Ireland. This is a story which is unique and specific, and not subject to easy generalisation or application to quite different situations.

ᘓ ᘓ ᘓ